ANGER
BUSTING
101

THE NEW ABCS FOR ANGRY MEN
AND
THE WOMEN WHO LOVE THEM

Newton Hightower

Bayou
Publishing

ANGER BUSTING 101

*THE NEW ABCS FOR ANGRY MEN
AND
THE WOMEN WHO LOVE THEM*

Newton Hightower

LMSW-ACP, LMFT, LPC, AAC
Director, Center for Anger Resolution, Inc.

Foreword
Donald S. Williamson, Ph.D.
Past President of The American Association for
Marriage and Family Therapy
and
Author of *The Intimacy Paradox*

Special Section on Medications for Angry Men
David C. Kay, M.D.
Medical Director, Center for Anger Resolution, Inc.

Printed in the United States of America

First Edition 10 9 8 7 6 5 4 3 2 1

Publisher's Cataloging-in-Publication
(Provided by Quality Books, Inc.)

Hightower, Newton.
   Anger busting 101 : the new ABCs for angry men and the women who love them / Newton Hightower ; foreword, Donald S. Williamson ; special section on medications for angry men, David C. Kay.
   p.cm.
   Includes bibliographical references and index.
   LCCN: 2001132541
   ISBN: 1-886298-04-01
   1. Anger. 2. Men--Psychology. 3. Man-woman relationships. I. Title.
BF575.A5H54 2002   152.4'7'081
                                      QB101-201216

Bayou Publishing
2524 Nottingham
Houston, TX 77005-1412
www.BayouPublishing.com
(713) 526-4558

Bayou
Publishing

"My purpose is to picture the cruelty of anger which not only vents its fury on a man here and there but rends in pieces whole nations."
— Seneca, Roman philosopher, 50 AD

PRAISE FOR *ANGER BUSTING 101*

"*Anger Busting 101* is a down-to-earth approach to handling anger and conflict in interpersonal relationships. It's full of lots of specific suggestions on how to handle your anger as well as suggestions for partners who are involved with angry people."
—Daniel Sonkin, Ph.D.
Author of *Learning to Live Without Violence: A Handbook for Men*

"*Anger Busting 101* is likely to become The Big Book for anger addicts. Newton Hightower is a pioneer in this long-neglected field of addiction. The ABCs he teaches in *Anger Busting 101* are the steps that will transform the lives of violent families."
—Blair Justice, Ph.D. and Rita Justice, Ph.D.
Psychologists and authors of *The Abusing Family*

"One of Newton's greatest attributes is his willingness to share his journey with those suffering and imprisoned by their anger. *Anger Busting 101* is a rich testament to a long traveled and well-studied road. His descriptions, understanding and explicit suggestions provide a long awaited footpath for others whose anger keeps them from living the lives they want and deserve. *Anger Busting 101* offers a chance of a new life to angry men and the women who love them."
—Karen Magee, M.A., LMFT
Jungian Analyst

"Mr. Hightower has merged his personal and clinical experiences to create an innovative approach to the treatment of rage, which offers hope to many and will result in a more peaceful world."
—Miriam M. Gottlieb, Ph.D.
Author of *The Angry Self*

"What a great book! This book is a real gift to men struggling to overcome the tyranny of anger in their lives!"
—Sam J. Buser, Ph.D.
President, Texas Psychological Association

"A practical guide for getting anger and your life under control."
—Bonnie Maslin, Ph.D.
Author of *The Angry Marriage*

"With humor and creativity Newton Hightower takes his twenty-five years of working successfully with angry and violent men and in simple easy-to-follow language, tells us how to effectively deal with our own out-of-control anger."

—Harvey Aronson, Ph.D.
Author of *Couch or Cushion? Buddhist Practice on Western Ground*

"Newton Hightower has provided therapists with an excellent resource for dealing with rage, an issue therapists often ignore or mishandle. His book, *Anger Busting 101*, provides strategies for dealing with the raging client and the family and friends affected by the rage. The book is readable, encouraging and specific about how to deal with raging clients, friends, spouses or family members. Traditional therapeutic practices have been ineffective and have contributed to a sense of failure and frustration in raging clients. This is required reading!"

—Penny D. Winkle, LMSW, LPCC, BCD
The Ohio State University–Counseling and Consultation Service

"*Anger Busting 101* has been created by someone who has been there. Newton Hightower speaks from the heart and passes on what he has learned through his own journey."
—David B. Wexler, Ph.D., Relationship Training Institute
Author of *Domestic Violence 2000*

"Hightower's real contribution lies not in showing rageaholics how to set limits on their 'toxic' anger but, more importantly, in providing a list of rage-incompatible behaviors that collectively lead to real inner peace."

—W. Doyle Gentry, Ph.D.
Author of *Anger-Free: Ten Basic Steps to Managing Your Anger*

"Newton exposes the myth of 'get it all out or stuff it' and offers a third alternative that stops the rage before it takes over. I've watched his methods work where I was certain they wouldn't."
—Lynn Bradley, Author of *Manic Depression: How to Live While Loving a Manic Depressive*

"This book is lively and full of solid information and great ideas."
—Bill O'Hanlon
Author of *Do One Thing Different*

"For the past 5 years I have enjoyed the challenge of leading anger therapy groups for women and men. Newton Hightower's approach is the best I have seen in the literature."
—Warren Holleman, Ph.D., Associate Professor, Baylor College of Medicine/ Director, Baylor Star of Hope Family Counseling Center

"Newton Hightower has it just right: he neither bludgeons nor coddles, but delivers a straightforward message, with enough humor and compassion to 'help the medicine go down' more easily. I will require this book for all my anger patients."
—Phil Bohnert, M.D., FAPA, Associate Professor of Psychiatry John A. Burns School of Medicine, University of Hawaii

"Newton explodes one of our most destructive psychological myths: 'Let your anger out or it will hurt you.' New brain research confirms his way is the best, and it should be required reading for therapists and couples."
—Carol Kelleher, Ph.D., Adjunct Professor, Univ. of Houston Grad. School of Social Work; Supervisor, Marriage / Family Therapists

"I work with the angriest people in the country—inmates. This book should be available to the counseling staff and to the inmates in jails and prisons nationwide."
—Thomas W. Baxter, M.A., Director of Corrections Houston Community College Northeast / Harris County Sheriff's Dept.

"The Newton Hightower method of 'Anger Busting' is undoubtedly the most effective method of controlling rage, saving marriages and lives. As a clinical psychologist of 30 years of practice, I think this book offers the opportunity for bringing about major behavioral changes—and within a brief time. This book is a must for all clinicians."
—Marian Yeager, Ph.D. Past President, Houston Psychological Association

"Most of us are afraid of anger. Not just the anger of others but our own as well. Newton Hightower isn't. In this book he takes the reader firmly by the hand and heart and leads us through scary territory so that we come out on the other side calmer and more confident about dealing with anger—both in ourselves and in others."
—Bill Kerley, Th.D., Methodist Clergyman Author of *What To Do While You Are Waiting for Things To Get Better*

"Tough, tender, and disarmingly funny, Newton Hightower opens readers up to the destructiveness of rage in men's lives, and points convincingly to its healing."

—Morris Taggart, Ph.D., Psychologist and Family Therapist
Former Board Member of American Family Therapy Association

"Newton Hightower provides a candid, provocative look at the devastating impact rage has on human life. His straightforward treatment approach provides hope to those who had all but given up on themselves. Reading this book may be the only chance rageaholics have to lead a normal life. I am proud to call him my mentor and friend."

—Jo Clancy, LMSW-ACP
Author of *Anger and Addiction: Breaking the Relapse Cycle*

"Angry, raging men are invariably unable to help themselves and, at the same time, experts at defeating the best efforts to help by others. They are in charge, but out of control! Here's a book that promises to break the deadlock—and delusions. Take this book home. Take it to your office. Take it to heart. You'll be challenged, and you'll be changed."

—John Hough, Ph.D.
Author of *Against the Wall*

"Finally a book is here that offers powerful, practical help for those whose lives have been damaged or destroyed by uncontrolled anger. While the principles are easy to read and understand, they are profoundly challenging and hopeful at the same time."

—Anne F. Grizzle, LMSW-ACP
Author of *Going Home Grown Up*

"Having witnessed Newton Hightower's program, I recommend it for anyone who has a problem with rage. It may not be the only solution, but it is the best I have seen."

—Bob Bradley
Author of *How to Survive Your Bipolar Brain and Stay Functional*

"Finally a book I'm comfortable giving both men and women; an essential guide for therapists to have in their office. It's useful for clinicians in every setting. A thought-provoking blend of philosophy, directives, and humor."

—Douglas T. Chan, Youth Enhancement Counselor
Houston Area Women's Center

"A no-nonsense approach that *will* help men who suffer from rage!"
—Paul Ekman, Ph.D., Professor of Psychology
University of California, San Francisco

"This is an easy read for the easily angered! And a must-read for anyone struggling to control their anger and a must-read for those trying to help them."
—Linda Walsh, Ph.D.
Psychologist

"This is a practical, focused method for stripping away destructive, decimating defenses and co-constructing a new and welcomed reality of love, respect, fun, intimacy, and growth! Newton has succeeded in distilling a graduate course in interpersonal relationships into an immediately utilizable trove of useful techniques for positive change."
—Harvey A. Rosenstock, M.D., FAPA
Co-author of *Journey Through Divorce*

"Newton Hightower delivers a straightforward message for angry men and the 'women who love them.' It is required reading for all my patients because the book offers hope, techniques and alternatives that are useful. This should be required reading for everyone living in our society."
—Andi H. Strauss, Ph.D., LCDC
Director, Traumatic Stress Institute

"I found it truly enjoyable to read this book. It was extremely easy, direct, and applicable. It's an easy step-by-step approach that I can give patients in therapy with me when they whine, "But, what am I supposed to 'do' to stop raging?!" I very much appreciated your personal story which makes the book an approach that is much more human."
—Jay D. Tarnow, M.D., FAPA
Tarnow Center for Self-Management SM

"I gave Newton's book to a male client who told me he never has had an anger problem. I asked him simply to skim it to help me figure out if it was any good from a man's perspective. The next time I saw him he had apologized to his wife and children for 30 years of rage. I think Newton is on to something."
—Leslye King Mize, Ph.D., Associate Professor & Director of Training,
Family Therapy Program- University of Houston Clear Lake

"Newton's new book, *Anger Busting 101*, gives powerless men the ultimate power: the power of choice and the freedom to use it. What a godsend for modern men and the women who love them."

—Rex McCaughtry, DCSW
Co-author of *Save the Males*

"Finally, we can quit wading through the litany of ineffective resources on anger management. Newton's book sets the record straight: read it and find a life-changing prescription for your anger and rage problems."

—John H. Morris, LMSW-ACP, LMFT
President, Houston Association for Marriage & Family Therapy

"This book offers healing and happiness to men who are addicted to rage and the verbal or physical expression of rage in violence."

—Donald S. Williamson, Ph.D.
Past President, American Association for Marriage & Family Therapy

"Newton provides an approach that helps with anger, when insight is not enough...this book is a manual for the individual who wants a direct path to the management and resolution of anger."

—Christian Restrepo, M.D., Certified Psychoanalyst
American Psychoanalytic Association

"Written from a 'no pain, no gain' approach, Newton's book will serve as a powerful Rageaholics's Bible for years to come."

—Ginger E. Blume, Ph.D.
Radio host/Newspaper columnist/Trainer/Psychologist

"In exposing his own sexism and power/control issues, Hightower progresses on his journey toward safety, equality, and justice for women. Moreover, he leads other men to that honorable goal."

—Toby Myers, Ed.D., Founder of the Pivot Project for Male Batterers
Honored as the Founder of the Battered Women's Movement in Texas

"Newton digs below cultural and professional myths/falsehoods to find out what is true and how to help in 'cursed darkness.'"

—Reverend J. Roland Cole, M.Div.
Counselor and Methodist Clergyman

"Newton Hightower uses his passion and experience to write a practical book that gives real solutions to a universal problem."

—Cardwell Nuckols, Ph.D.
Coauthor of *Healing an Angry Heart*

DEDICATION

To Donna Hightower, my wife, who with a soft, determined voice turned a pit bull into a cocker spaniel.

To Alisa Hightower, my daughter, who with spontaneity and determination became a remarkable woman.

To LaVona Hightower, my mother, to whom I owe my life and my sense of humor, which has saved my life.

ACKNOWLEDGMENTS

A long-time fishing buddy called me during the Christmas holidays to see what I was doing. I said, "I am getting ready to make a set of six tapes to help rageful men and their wives."

He said, "If you can make a set of tapes, then that is a sign that you are ready to write your book." He had been on this "write your book" theme for several years.

I said, "This is not a good time for me to get into that. Let's just go to lunch. I don't want to discuss a book."

He said, "How does Chinese food sound? By the way, bring a legal pad and a pen."

My fishing and lunch buddy is Terrell Dixon, who at that time was chairman of the English Department at the University of Houston. This was an example of someone believing in me when I did not believe in myself. Terrell helped me with an outline and a title which formed the basis of this book. I still have the legal pad with soy sauce stains.

Most of all, I would like to acknowledge my wife, Donna Hightower, who in the first few years of our marriage told me the things I was going to have to quit doing and things I needed to start doing if I wanted to stay married to her. This began as a list of 10 behaviors to abstain from but grew over a period of several years to 20. Donna was specific and behavioral, which made change possible for the first time in my life.

I want to acknowledge Morris Taggart, the therapist Donna took me to when she could not get through to me. Morris was never intimidated by my self-righteous outbursts but kept asking me, "So what is it that *you* could change?" He just wouldn't buy that it was her fault I was losing my temper.

I want to thank my long-term friend, mentor, former therapist and consultant, Donald Williamson, for sticking with me for the last 16 years. He believed so much more was possible for me than I could even imagine for myself. After my second divorce, I used to argue with him that he didn't understand how defective I was in relationships. He laughed, shook his head and said, "You *used* to have a problem. Now you are capable of a finer intimacy than you ever dreamed possible."

Gail Donohue Storey, author of the highly praised novels *The Lord's Motel* and *God's Country Club,* was the first to review an incredibly rough transcription of my tapes, which I thought was almost ready to send to a publisher. Gail ever so gently informed me that it was going to need a "little cleaning up," but thought I had a best seller. Looking back, I can't believe I was lucky enough to have found someone with such a gift for tact and encouragement.

Howard Karger read the manuscript after six months of my working on it. Howard is the director of the doctoral program in social work at the University of Houston. He has published 10 books on social policy. Howard was honest when he said, "I think you are onto something here, but it really needs a lot of work." Thank you for all the hours of work you put into this book to make it readable and "user friendly" (your favorite phrase).

Victor Loos, my publisher and friend. It is a pleasure to work with someone who understands my vision. Thank you for taking a risk on me. Also thank you for tolerating the rough edges in my personality as well as my writing.

Deborah Shelton, my editor. Your enthusiasm for the book kept my spirit going. Your willingness to listen and help when I was stuck kept the writing moving.

CONTENTS

FOREWORD

I am delighted to write a foreword for this stimulating and enlightening book by Newton Hightower.

The book offers a way to healing and happiness to men who are addicted to rage and the verbal or physical expression of rage in violence. This is an area of such emotional toxicity and discomfort that most psychotherapists are inclined to sidestep it. But to his credit and to the benefit of others, Newton has found a calling here. This is a congruent book because the author is a congruent man. What you see is what you get.

The author's method is built on the presupposition that whatever the pain in a man's personal past, however deep his wound in the present and however provocative, contributory and complex the current social context of a man's life may be, there is no hope for the rageaholic unless and until he takes total responsibility for his rageful behavior. The motivation to change, Newton proposes, is usually dependent on the impact and the certainty of the punitive consequences in a man's life if he does not change his behavior. He makes a compelling argument.

What makes this book both gripping and effective is the fact that Newton Hightower has himself made the journey of which he speaks. He practices what he preaches and embodies the values he extols. This is rare, not just among psychotherapists, but among us human beings as a whole. The book is earthy, raw, immediate and practical, just what the doctor ought to be ordering. All of us can find ourselves on these pages to one degree or another.

This book is innocent of idealism yet is ringing with hope and possibility for recovery in every chapter. This engaging paradox makes the book so appealing. Such an unromantic book could only have been written by an incurable romantic. And that is good news. As Newton shows, the rageaholic can retrain his behavior and learn not to express rage destructively without losing his passion for life. I admire and commend to the reader both this book and its author, who now shares the fruit of his own learning with a community desperately searching for help.

Toward the conclusion of the book, Newton declares that this is ultimately a journey of spiritual transformation. We are all on the same trip—no exceptions. Paths may vary, but for those for whom managing rage is a core challenge—read on. There is hope.

—Donald S. Williamson, Ph.D.
Leadership Institute of Seattle, March 2001

PREFACE

"Out-of-hand anger ruins many lives. More, I believe, than schizo-phrenia, more than alcohol, more than AIDS. Maybe even more than depression."

—Seligman and Seligman,
What You Can Change...and What You Can't

"Is there help and hope for the angry man?"

You did it. You have picked up a book that describes a method that has been used successfully to help thousands of men overcome their problems with anger. This method offers hope in addition to practical, step-by-step, here-is-how-to-do-it advice for ending your difficulties with anger. By reading this book, you can start changing today and start making the progress you desire at a pace you feel comfortable with.

You may find it impossible to believe that a single book could ever help solve a problem as serious and life-damaging as anger and rage. You may already have read several self-help books on anger and may be in counseling now. You may find counseling quite satis-fying, but when it comes to the bottom line, you are raging as much as ever. What's to say, then, that this book is any different from what you have already tried or may be trying now? Well, read on and see.

You may have been told that you are going to have to take psy-cho-archaeology expeditions back to your childhood to discover and piece together the various elements that may be causing your anger problem. That may be helpful—or it may be a way to avoid chang-ing your behavior. Some new clients tell me, "I know I need to work through my issues with my mother and father and that it will take a few years." I worry that in the meantime they may be divorced,

17

fired, in prison, or dead if they can't change their angry ways sooner. You can change right now.

Wrong ABCs

Growing up, I somehow mislearned my ABCs. I expressed myself and lived by *Anger*, *Blame* and *Criticism*. These ABCs couldn't support me or my relationships. Many failures and a great deal of pain taught me new ABCs: *Abstaining*, *Believing* and *Communicating*. This is my personal story of what it took to develop a better way to live.

My Personal Journey

In 1984 I was 40 years old and my second marriage was going downhill fast. Our fights were getting more frequent and more violent. I was ashamed that I could not stop my own rage and violence, so I consulted with three highly respected therapists during this time.

At the end of the initial session, the first one told me that my marital situation was impossible and that I needed a lawyer, not a therapist. I did not go back to him. The second therapist met with me twice. I explained to him that I would go to any lengths to save my marriage. He suggested that we have joint sessions with my wife and me together.

During one marital session, we got into a screaming match that quickly turned violent. The therapist kept saying that the session was over. He told us to leave immediately. After my wife finally left the office, the therapist recommended that we get a divorce. Furthermore, he stated emphatically that he was not going to work with us. He said that it was the only physical violence that had occurred in his office in over 30 years. Furthermore, many of those 30 years were spent working with drug addicts.

At that time in my professional life, I worked as a group and family therapist on the Inpatient Drug Abuse Unit of the Veterans Administration Medical Center. I volunteered to start a group for veterans with rage problems. I taught them expressive techniques to get their feelings out. We met together for an hour every day to yell and scream and pound pillows. After the group met for a week, Dr. David Kay, the director of the unit, called me into his office. He said that the men in my group were losing their temper and getting discharged from the unit due to verbal abuse of staff and fellow patients at an even greater rate than ever. Many of the men were on parole and would go to prison if they did not complete our program.

He pointed out that they were motivated, but my techniques were just not working. I explained that I needed more time to get to the underlying rage at their parents and that once that was expressed, they would be calmer. All I needed was another week.

Two weeks later Dr. Kay called me back into his office. "Newton, I don't know what you are doing in that anger group to try to help those men with their rage problems, but whatever it is, it is making them *worse*. If we keep going at this rate, we won't have any patients left on the unit. Your anger group is disbanded."

That statement was my wake-up call. What I had been doing for my own rage problem, as well as my clients' rage, had made our problems worse. I proved wrong those people who believe that angry men can never change. I showed that I could make them change—for the worse. The experience served as a catalyst to find a way to help men change—for the better.

The next day I received a professional journal that had an article about battering men by Jeffrey Edleson, who had started a self-help group for male batterers on the East Coast. I called him and ordered the manual for this group. Also in that journal was a book advertisement for *The Hitting Habit* by Jeanne Deschner. I called and ordered the book. Shortly after receiving it, I got a flyer advertising a workshop by Jeanne Deschner in a nearby city.

I drove 200 miles to go to her training workshop for therapists. Deschner's approach to domestic violence had a clear plan for recovery and it was *not* about expressing anger and getting it all out. Neither was it about learning to express anger appropriately. I had earlier discovered that every time I tried to express my anger "appropriately," I ended up breaking furniture.

I spoke to Jeanne after the meeting and expressed my excitement about her methods. We made plans to do a joint presentation at a national conference the following year, which would focus on group therapy for angry and violent men. We presented a well-attended workshop in Washington, D.C. in February of 1985.

Jeanne recommended the first book written for abusive men, *Learning to Live without Violence*[1] by Daniel Sonkin and Michael Durphy. With this workbook in hand, I was able to restart my anger management groups back at the Veterans Administration Hospital.

When I returned to Houston, I made a therapy appointment with Rita Justice, the third therapist I sought out. She and her husband, Blair Justice, wrote *Abusing Families*, a classic in the field of child abuse treatment. Although her work focused on child abuse, I thought she might be able to help me. I could not find anyone outside the court system who worked with abusive men.

Rita was sympathetic to my anger problem and my goal of saving my marriage. She had not heard of Jeanne Deschner's book but liked the ideas and was willing to read it and work with me using that model. I went into group therapy with Rita and we met occasionally for marital therapy. I learned about "time-outs" and when the sessions would get too intense for me, I would leave the room for a few minutes. Eventually I saw that I could not save the marriage at my rate of progress without my wife's help, but she refused further counseling. I got divorced for the second time. I was devastated and ashamed.

My Mission

My mission since that time has been to create a program of therapy that works for men in the same predicament I was in—men who want to save their marriage, but when they go to therapy are either told they are hopeless, the marriage is hopeless or it is going to take five years of therapy to make a change or, even worse, they are told that they need to express their anger and get it all out.

There are men who want to stop their fault-finding, sarcasm, arguing, self-justification and self-righteous indignation, rage and violence. There are men who do not want to be divorced and lose their families. They want to be able to say, like I have for the last 10 years, "I am happily married and my life is good."

This book is for the men stuck in the same jam and for the women who could love them again.

The Destructive Aspects of Anger

"We are here to encounter the most outrageous, brutal, dangerous and intractable of all passions; the most loathsome and unmannerly; nay, the most ridiculous too; and the subduing of this monster will do a great deal toward the establishment of human peace."
—Seneca, Roman philosopher, 50 AD

Anger causes a bodily reaction. Your sympathetic nervous system and muscles mobilize for physical attack. Your muscles tense and your blood pressure and heart rate skyrocket. Your digestive processes stop. Certain brain centers are triggered, which then change your brain chemistry. When you are angry, your bodily functions change for the worse. Dr. Charles Cole, Colorado State University, found that the physiological effects of anger can cause blood vessels to constrict, increase heart rate and blood pressure, and eventually lead to the destruction of heart muscle. After studying the reactions to stress and anger in more than 800 patients, Dr. Cole concluded that every thought has a physiological consequence.[2]

Looking at the effects of anger, Dr. Leo Maddow, chairman of the Department of Psychiatry and Neurology at the University of Pennsylvania, observed that brain hemorrhages are usually caused by a combination of hypertension and cerebral arteriosclerosis. He found that anger can produce the hypertension which explodes the diseased cerebral artery, resulting in a stroke. Not only does anger produce physical symptoms ranging from headaches to hemorrhoids, it can also seriously aggravate already existing physical illnesses. "Someone who stays angry long after the particular incident that caused the anger may be committing slow suicide," summarizes Lance Morrow, who found that his own internalized anger twice threatened his life by causing a heart attack.[3]

Each episode of anger or hostility sets off a physiological response in your body causing your heart to beat faster, your blood pressure to rise, your coronary arteries to narrow, and your blood to become thicker. When the blood becomes thicker, the heart has to work harder to pump it. For people with heart disease, this reaction can reduce blood flow to the heart, creating a potentially fatal condition.[4]

A study done by Dr. Ichiro Kawachi, of the Harvard School of Public Health, examined about 1,300 older men (average age of 62) over a seven-year period. Dr. Kawachi found that those men with the highest levels of anger were three times more likely to develop heart disease than men with the lowest levels of anger.[5]

Other researchers at Union Memorial Hospital and Loyola College of Maryland in Baltimore interviewed 41 patients who just had angioplasties to unclog arteries. Those who scored highest in hostility ("Hostile Type A") were 2.5 times more likely to need repeat angioplasty within the year. Furthermore, contrary to the common advice from friends and therapists to "get it all out" when angry, verbally berating partners or expressing hostility toward other people only serves to compromise physical health.[6] Let one of my former clients tell you in his own words the price he paid and what *finally* worked for him.

The Story of Jim R.

My family has a long and violent tradition. My grandfather shot and killed an unarmed man in a small Oklahoma town after they got into an argument. The grand jury didn't charge him because he was the only dentist in town and because, "the man needed killing anyway."

My father killed a man before I was born, but I was never clear on the story. He was not charged because it was self-defense. In second grade, my father and older brothers mocked me when I came home beaten up by some older boys. The next day the older boys came after me again. This time I ran home to get my brother's pistol. When I showed up with the gun, they scattered. After hearing the story, my father and brother thought it was funny and admired my "guts."

Although I had fought all of my life, I had never hit my wife or children, but I was verbally abusive and intimidated them.

I've been stabbed and shot. Both times I charged at men who were holding weapons. Both times I almost died. Once I beat a man almost to death. I thought I would feel remorse standing over him, but I did not. I kicked him several times more in the head and left him to die. He survived. Even after I quit drinking and got on lithium for my manic-depressive illness, my rage problem continued. It seemed to have a life of its own. I'm now 65 years old and on probation for choking my 20-year-old granddaughter. She'd been yelling at my wife and refused to shut up. As she lay there on the floor unconscious, I thought I had killed her. I never felt such overwhelming fear and shame in my life. That moment helped change my life.

My granddaughter was physically okay. However, I was arrested and my wife left me. My adult children refused to speak to me. I was referred by my psychiatrist to a men's anger group that used the ABC method. I was skeptical at first about changing such a life-long habit at my age.

The recovery model made sense to me since I am a recovering alcoholic. I began treating my anger as I had my desire to drink 25 years before...I simply did not give in to the impulse to express anger, no matter what. As we say in A.A.

"...even if my ass fell off." I used the Abstain, Believe and Communicate method.

One of the crucial steps for me was turning off my violent fantasy life. I have learned to change the channel that plays violent revenge fantasies. I abstain from violent fantasies just as I do from romantic drinking fantasies. I distract myself. I force myself to repeat prayers or phrases over and over—sometimes out loud if I am in the car. I think of pleasant scenes, real or imagined. Sometimes I will just pick up something and force myself to read it to get the channel changed.

This has been the third biggest turning point in my life. Giving up drinking was the first; getting on lithium for my manic-depressive illness was the second. Now I have given up expressing rage and anger completely. My wife noticed the change and came back home. All but one of my children are speaking to me. I now can do what I never thought possible: Lose. Be wrong. Walk away quietly. If I can do it, so can you.

What if nothing else has worked?

"What if nothing else has worked?" you may ask. "Can the new ABC method even help me?" I know it can be very discouraging to have tried and failed to overcome an anger or rage problem. Please know, however, that you are not alone.

During my own life, I have been fired, divorced and depressed. I have had a long history of rage problems that set me on many paths looking for solutions. I pounded pillows for years and meditated daily for over a decade, both to no avail. I now present the path I found that worked for me after everything else had failed. It is my life's mission to bring this message to other men who suffer from the same problem.

The majority of ragers experience some degree of failure while trying to find a strategy that works for them. Can the new ABC method help you? The answer is an unqualified *yes, if you follow the instructions.* It's *yes,* even if you have been violent all your life and have never been in a relationship in which you were not abusive. It's *yes,* even if your wife has been told at the battered women's shelter that you cannot change and that men like you get worse over time. It's *yes,* even if every therapist your wife saw recommended she leave you. You *can* change quickly, dramatically, and forever.

It is critical to try something different if what you have
been doing hasn't worked.

What if I don't think I have an anger problem?

Perhaps you are not reading this book because you think you
have an anger problem. Maybe you are one of those people who are
reading this book because someone close to you—your spouse, a
parent, a child–thinks you have a problem with anger. Maybe you
are reading this book as part of a program you have been forced to
attend.

Being in counseling or in a program may not be your idea. You
may believe that others are your biggest problem. Your spouse may
be threatening to divorce you, your employer may have given you a
final warning, or the judge is giving you a choice between jail and
counseling.

Perhaps what you believe is that you were in the wrong place at
the wrong time. Your wife or girlfriend may have called the police
after both of you were scuffling over the keys, and she is the one
who fell and skinned her elbows...but you were the one who went
to jail.

Can the method described in this book help you in these kinds of
circumstances? What if you don't think you have an anger problem?

Believe it or not, the method described in this book can help.
Almost all of my experience has been in working with men who
have been under some kind of external pressure to be in a men's
anger management group. Many of these are men on probation for
domestic violence or their wives gave them the choice between my
men's group and divorce court.

The ABC method helps you develop successful
strategies for dealing with the people who have had it
with your rageful behavior.

My experience has taught me something you probably already know: Simply biding your time in a counseling group may work for a while, but eventually those close to you will want to see results. They will not stop complaining until they see some evidence that you are at least trying. The ABC method can help you change your situation and help you meet the demands of others. You can accomplish this while simultaneously maintaining your dignity and independence.

What does destructive anger do?

Destructive anger hurts your health, makes you miserable, blocks solutions, wastes your energy, keeps you helpless, invites attacks, imprisons your spirit, wrecks human relations, gives you headaches, causes accidents, ruins restful sleep and turns a love life into a lonely life. You may need to go ahead and add as many casualties as you can think of until you are completely convinced that rage is a punishing, not a rewarding, thrill.

There is an opportunity for men with anger and rage problems to learn a new alphabet, different from the one they were taught growing up. If you are a man who tries hard to control your temper and has good intentions but just finds yourself blowing up, it may be that you need to learn some new ABCs. The old ABCs you learned in your childhood—"Anger, Blame and Criticism" —are not helping your life and marriage work. These new ABCs have to do with a whole new perspective and a whole new way of life—so new that if you are a man with a rage problem, you have probably never spoken some of the phrases you will practice in this book.

Yet these new phrases have helped hundreds of men in the last 15 years save their marriages, their jobs and, in some cases, stay out of prison and save their lives. I have trained therapists all across the country in these techniques. They work. My goal for you is not just to stop blowing up but to have a happy marriage and a happy life.

There is a way out of destructive anger.

INTRODUCTION

Are you addicted to anger?

In the mid-1980s John Bradshaw, author of *Healing the Shame That Binds You*, wrote about "rageaholics," those of us who are addicted to anger and rage. The model made sense to me. I worked with rageful drug addicts and I began to think of anger as if it were a drug. As I did more reading, I found that there actually are biochemical changes in our bodies when we rage, use profanity or pound things. Those of us who rage a lot have more health problems than people who practice containing their anger. The popular psychological theories that suggested a need to express anger for mental and physical health reasons have been proven false when put under the microscope of scientific research. The more we scream and yell, the worse our health gets, the more prone we are to heart attacks and the worse our rage problem becomes.

"Sure I get angry. Doesn't everybody?" This book is certainly not for all men. Some men may need to learn to express their anger, but others have become addicted to the expression of anger just like the alcoholic has become addicted to alcohol. As with the alcoholic, solemn oaths to use willpower to "control ourselves" have failed repeatedly. Still, we continue trying to do more of what has not worked.

If you have unsuccessfully tried willpower, solemn oaths, stopping drinking, marital therapy, getting all the anger out once and for all, exploring anger at your father, learning the appropriate expression of anger, meditation and some medication, you may be convinced that there is no way to stop the destructive power of anger. You may be beginning to lose your marriage, children, jobs and

27

friends. You may be caught in the grip of an addiction even stronger
than you realized. You may be a rageaholic.

> Instead of trying still more willpower and more
> eloquent oaths, it may be time to try another approach
> that has worked for many men.

"I thought it was healthy to express my anger." For the last 50
years the world has been saying, "Express yourself." "Let it out."
"It's good for you to express your feelings." "It's bad for you to
repress your feelings."

Seymour Feshbach, an early pioneer in anger research, explored
hostility and aggressiveness by taking a group of young boys who
were not especially aggressive or destructive and encouraging them
to kick furniture and play with violent toys. They did so enthusiasti-
cally. Instead of draining these boys of aggression, the aggressive
"play" actually increased it. The boys became more rather than less
hostile and destructive. As opposed to letting off steam, expressing
hostility toward another person may increase rather than decrease
hostile feelings.

My work agrees with Feshbach, and it has led to this radical
principle: *Abstain from the expression of anger.* As background for
this alternative approach to dealing with anger, let me first develop
in more detail the two theories of anger that have dominated the
past century.

Two Theories on Anger Resolution: "Build-up/Blow-up" and "Expressive Anger"

One way to consider anger is what I call the "Build-up/Blow-up
Theory of Anger." At the turn of the century Freud relied on the
popular scientific theory of his day, hydraulic theory, to explain how
psychic energy worked. In hydraulic theory, a pressure or force is
either released or it causes pressure in some other part of the system.
Let me use the example of a pressure cooker to link anger and
hydraulic theory. Imagine a pressure cooker with a flame underneath
and the pressure building up. The steam inside the cooker is equiva-
lent to anger and one of the ways to release the steam is to take the
lid off the pressure cooker. As a child, I used to ask my mother when
she cooked chicken and vegetables in the pressure cooker to please

take off the lid so we could eat our lunch. She said it was dangerous to take off the lid too soon. She ran cold water on it and I begged her again. Finally, out of frustration, she took the lid off, steam rushed out, and she got burned.

"Maybe if I get it all out, I will be okay?" Those of us with anger problems may be encouraged to express our anger. We may be told that it is good to get it out. We might be told that anger can even harm us physically if we don't express it. Many who believe in the hydraulic theory of anger even suggest a big release (catharsis) for anger.

> The Build-Up/Blow-Up approach to therapy maintains that if we take the lid off and let out the steam, there will be no pressure building up and then we won't be getting angry at people in our everyday life. We will have released the anger.

Expressive therapy, often associated with encounter groups and psychodrama, encourages the pounding of pillows, yelling and screaming or psychodrama with players representing people in your past that you are angry at. In psychodrama, you are encouraged to yell and tell these people how you really feel. The cathartic model in psychotherapy was the first path I chose in my attempt to get the destructive aspects of my anger under control. In Los Angeles in the late 1960s and early 1970s, proponents of this model believed that our culture had been too restrictive about anger. We needed to "let it out" and "express ourselves." "Let those feelings out!" the facilitators would cheer me on as I screamed my rage.

This approach was believed to be a good antidote to the leftover repression of the Victorian era. The idea was that we could heal and become whole if we just let ourselves go and trusted our impulses.

There was value in this model for me and there still is value for many men in cathartic expression—pounding pillows and screaming profanity until exhaustion. The value can be to become less afraid of our anger, to experience the underlying feelings of grief. Often, tender yearnings hide beneath the rage. Sobbing comes after the screaming. The guilt about anger, hatred and rage dissolves to some extent when the rage outburst is accepted and welcomed by a therapy group. Crying in the arms of loving people and being held afterward can be a very satisfying experience. However, the research evidence does not support that using this model in any way reduces rage outbursts during the rest of our lives.

No matter how good and nurturing the cathartic experience was, my anger outbursts only got worse during this time.

> The more anger we rageaholics express, the more we have to express.

"I've been told that I need to learn to express my anger appropriately." Again, let's imagine a pressure cooker, but instead of taking off the lid, let's set the pressure valve to slowly release the steam when it reaches a certain intensity. For example, we might say to our spouse, "I have some feelings of resentment toward you" or "Your behavior in the last few days has created some growing feelings of resentment" or "I would just like to let you know that I am feeling angry toward you because of your behavior last night at the party."

The idea is that we can express anger in a contained, appropriate way, and let the steam out gradually. Many of those who rage have been to therapists who think we haven't been taught how to express our anger appropriately; the therapy begins by attempting to teach us the appropriate expression of anger. If the "appropriate expression of anger" is used around resentment issues in a structured way, some of us can use it beneficially.

Following my experience with expressive therapies, I thought learning this appropriate expression approach was the answer for me, so I began learning, then teaching, the appropriate expression of anger. My wife said I was an excellent teacher and could do well in role plays, but even though I knew it in my head, when the adrenaline rush hit, I was gone. Typically I would start by saying, "Sweetheart, I would like to sit down and share with you after dinner." (That's called making an appointment—which is good.) Then, when we got comfortable, I would say, "I have been feeling angry and resentful about some things."

She would say, "What?"

I would reply, "What? You don't even know what?" and then I would go into a rage. She said I did well for up to 30 seconds but could never get past that.

> The "appropriate expression of anger" for me and many of us was just a prelude to one more tantrum. I had to face it—I could teach it, but I just couldn't do it.

A Different Theory of Anger: Rage as an Addiction

An alternative theory from the first two theories of anger is the "abstain," "dissolve" or "containment theory of anger." It suggests we leave the lid on the pressure cooker, keep the valve closed, and *turn off the fire underneath it.* Now, what happens if the pressure cooker just stays there? If we let the pressure cooker stand there long enough and we take the lid off, there is no steam. Steam equals anger in this image, so if you just let the pressure cooker (us) sit there, the steam turns into something else—cool water.

> Cool water in the bottom of the pressure cooker is what we angry men need to have.

"When angry, I don't say anything?" It will take some work and practice to keep the lid on; it is hard not to let a little steam seep out of the pressure valve and not to take the lid off. The idea is to keep the lid on tight, and to let the anger turn back into peace.

In the 1970s some authors suggested that we have a "Vesuvius Hour." Vesuvius is a volcano in Italy that erupted and buried the thriving city of Pompeii. The idea was that when we got home, rather than having a cocktail hour, we would erupt like a volcano, scream and yell, and call our spouse and children ugly names. Our children and spouse, in turn, would call us names, yell and scream. Everybody would get their aggression out for the day and have a peaceful, wonderful evening. But we know now that this practice actually aggravates the feelings and intensity of anger. The research that documents how anger makes our health and relationship problems worse is reviewed in *Anger Kills*[7] by Redford and Virginia Williams.

Carol Tavris[8] in her comprehensive study, *Anger: The Misunderstood Emotion* corrects some common misconceptions about expressing anger:

> *Myth #1:* "Aggression is the instinctive catharsis for anger."
>
> *Reality:* Aggression is an acquired cathartic habit, a learned reaction practiced by people who think they can get away with behaving this way.
>
> *Myth #2:* "Talking out anger gets rid of it—or at least makes you feel less angry."
>
> *Reality:* A series of studies indicates that the overt expression of anger can increase it. Tavris suggests that before speaking out, evaluate whether you want to stay angry or not.
>
> *Myth #3:* "Tantrums and other childhood rages are healthy expressions of anger that forestall neuroses."
>
> *Reality:* As Tavris states, "The emotions are as subject to the laws of learning as any other behavior."

Tantrums, which peak at two and three years of age, begin to wane by age four unless the child learns to control others through such behavior.

What are the signs that rage has turned into an addiction?

All addictions have symptoms, which allow us to recognize these problems as addictive diseases. The signs of addictive diseases are self-stimulation, compulsion, obsession, denial, withdrawal and craving syndrome, and unpredictable behavior. Like alcoholism or drug use, anger meets many of the criteria.

Self-Stimulation. For those of us who are rageaholics, expressing our anger is self-stimulating. It triggers our compulsion for more anger. For example, let's pretend that we are going to provide treatment for alcoholics. On the way to the treatment center we stop and buy a case of beer. When we get there, we tell the alcoholics in therapy that they just need to do a lot of drinking to get it out of their system once and for all. This, I believe, is similar to when therapists tell men with rage problems, "You just need to express yourself and get it out of your system." It is just as absurd.

The more alcoholics drink, the more they want. The more we ragers rage, the more we want to rage. One way to define alcoholism is that when the alcoholic ingests alcohol, it sets up a self-stimulating system in which he craves more alcohol. The more alcohol a person drinks, the more alcohol that person wants. It is the same way with rageaholics.

Compulsion. Anger addiction or "rageaholism" is the compulsive pursuit of a mood change by repeatedly engaging in episodes of rage despite adverse consequences. Rageaholics are individuals who continue to rage compulsively without regard to the negative consequences. It is the compulsion that signals the disease of addiction. Despite all judgment, reason, insight or consequence, we continue to use "the substance" compulsively.[9]

> Compulsion or loss of control is the inability to stop expressing anger once we have begun. The inability to control angry words is a certain sign of rageaholism. Loss of control—that is addiction.

When we can no longer control how much or when we rage, we have crossed the line into addiction. Brief periods of abstinence from rage may occur because of guilt or concern about the loss of a mate or of a job, but eventually, despite the best of intentions to control our tongue and hands, the rageaholic will be off again on another tantrum.

When control is lost, we ragers have entered into a crucial phase of addiction and may never again be able to return to the controlled expression of anger. Once this point is reached, we cannot predict what will set us off or how far we will go with our behavior. Our behavior is often as puzzling to us as it is to those around us.

> There is a paradox to all addictions. Addicts rage,
> drink, drug or eat compulsively in an effort to feel
> inherently better, but instead we feel worse.

Addicts will try anything to solve the problem except to stay away from the substance or behavior that triggers the addiction. Once the compulsion is triggered, all efforts at control fail.

In all forms of addiction, the control over thoughts and behavior is lost. As addiction progresses, our losses become increasingly profound and our life is no longer under our control. We are at the mercy of anyone who provokes us. Our thought processes become dominated by the addiction and we look for opportunities to indulge our addiction. Anger, revenge and rage take over. Our life becomes a booby trap, baited with pride and vengefulness as we wait for someone to offend us in some real or imagined way. As one client said, "I used to have trouble going to sleep at night because it would take me two or three hours to imagine killing everybody who had ever pissed me off, so I could fall asleep."

Obsession. Rageaholics are frequently preoccupied with resentment and fantasies of revenge. Those thoughts sometimes rise powerfully and allow no other thoughts to enter. No matter how hard we try to stop them, ideas of outrage and revenge predominate. The force of anger is sometimes irresistible and followed by action. Therefore, the preoccupation with the "wrongs" of others and revenge continually leads to rage. Progressively, these thoughts crowd out all others until our life becomes chronically revenge oriented. At that point, anger controls our thoughts.

> It is a psychological truth that we move toward our
> dominant thought.

Denial. Denial keeps anger addicts trapped. It is the mental process by which we conclude that the addiction is not the problem— it's *them.* Ignorance of addiction and the inability to examine ourselves work together to keep anger addicts stuck. Knowing no other way to live, we deny that there is anything wrong with us. This system of denial ensures that the process of rage and righteous indignation will continue. It is the speck-and-log-in-the-eye confusion problem. "Take the log out of your own eye before trying to take the speck out of your neighbor's eye," Jesus admonished.[10] Yes, we ragers are right; there may be a speck in our wife's eye, the other driver may indeed be wrong. But our focus should be on the log in our eye—that rage.

> Righteous indignation keeps our focus off of ourselves. This is why we ragers seldom are able to say, "I am wrong."

Withdrawal and Craving. As with any addiction, anger has a detoxification period. This is a very vulnerable time when addicts often feel unreal, like we have given up "who we are." Craving is high during this time. Those who abstain from name-calling, profanity and yelling during this period report more depression than usual for the first three months. Afterward, however, if we have achieved complete abstinence and maintained it for 90 days, we find we no longer think in profane or disparaging terms. It may even become shocking when we hear others do it.

Often in an anger hangover, we feel that we can probably do what it takes to live the rest of our lives without expressing anger— and without violence, verbal or physical. Typically, during the first 90 days of abstinence, ragers feel vulnerable and spend a lot of time thinking and hoping for a situation that will allow us to use violence for some heroic purpose. These heroic rescue fantasies are a symptom of our craving for anger like the heroin addict craves a fix. We are restless soldiers hoping for what Teddy Roosevelt called a "nice little war."

It may be time for us to "beat our spears into plowshares." Many of us were trained to be soldiers by our culture through physical contact sports and the military. It got into our blood and hasn't yet gotten out. It is interesting to ask ourselves when we last needed physical violence or the threat of physical violence to prevent injury to ourselves or someone else. For me, the answer is something like 45 years. All those chivalrous violent fantasies we think we need to protect us and our families from robbers and murderers need to go. In fact, our family is actually in much greater danger from us than some external threat. Constantly rehearsing break-ins and car jack-ings will not help us in our recovery.

> The statistics show that the person most likely to injure our wife is us, not a burglar or robber. We rageful men have met the enemy—and he is us.

Unpredictable Behavior. Another definition of alcoholism is that when an alcoholic drinks, there is no way to predict his or her behavior. He may drink appropriately from time to time, just as the rageaholic may express anger appropriately from time to time. However, when the alcoholic starts to drink alcohol, all bets are off. No one knows what is going to happen. He or she may drink appro-priately or may disappear for days. When rageaholics start to express anger, no one knows where it is going to go. The most likely thing is that we are going to explode, rant and rave. How can we then relate to "the appropriate expression" of anger?

We rageaholics would like to learn how to express our anger appropriately just like alcoholics would like to learn how to drink appropriately. But can we be taught to do this? Yes, you can be taught, but when the adrenaline hits, it's an excuse to blow up. We keep arguing that we are expressing ourselves appropriately. While there are some exceptions, I encourage those with rage problems to abstain from the expression of anger for one year.

Remember, this plan is only for that small percent of the popula-tion who have rage or violence problems. (The approach described here is not for everyone.) For those addicted to anger, it won't work to express our anger. We have tried it and know it has never worked. Many of us have been to therapy for years and have worked very hard at learning to express our anger appropriately. However, we often feel frustrated and don't know why we can't learn it. In fact, we may feel relieved when we decide it is all right to give up trying to express our anger appropriately and begin to learn how to abstain from the expression of anger altogether.

Do you have an anger problem? A Self-Assessment Test

Answer true or false to the following questions. Please be honest, not a "lip-service honest," but fearlessly and searchingly honest. There is much to gain and you don't have to share the results with anyone but yourself.

Anger Self-Assessment Test

T F 1. I've had trouble on the job because of my temper.

T F 2. People say that I fly off the handle easily.

T F 3. I don't always show my anger, but when I do, look out.

T F 4. I still get angry when I think of the bad things people did to me in the past.

T F 5. I hate lines, and I especially hate waiting in line.

T F 6. I often find myself engaged in heated arguments with the people who are close to me.

T F 7. At times I've felt angry enough to kill.

T F 8. When someone says or does something that upsets me, I don't usually say anything at the time, but later I spend a lot of time thinking of cutting replies I could and should have made.

T F 9. I find it very hard to forgive someone who has done me wrong.

T F 10. I get angry with myself when I lose control of my emotions.

T F 11. I get aggravated when people don't behave the way they should.

T F 12. If I get really upset about something, I have a tendency to feel sick later (frequently experiencing weak spells, headaches, upset stomach or diarrhea).

T F 13. When things don't go my way, I "lose it."

T F 14. I am apt to take frustration so badly that I cannot put it out of my mind.

T F 15. I've been so angry at times I couldn't remember what I said or did.

T F 16. Sometimes I feel so hurt and alone that I've thought about killing myself.

T F 17. After arguing with someone, I despise myself.

T F 18. When riled, I often blurt out things I later regret saying.

T F 19. Some people are afraid of my bad temper.

T F 20. When I get angry, frustrated or hurt, I comfort myself by eating or using alcohol or other drugs.

T F 21. When someone hurts me, I want to get even.

T F 22. I've gotten so angry at times that I've become physically violent, hitting other people or breaking things.

T F 23. I sometimes lie awake at night thinking about the things that upset me during the day.

T F 24. People I've trusted have often let me down, leaving me feeling angry or betrayed.

T F 25. I'm an angry person. My temper has already caused lots of problems, and I need help changing it.

Scoring the Anger Self-Assessment Test. If you answered true to 10 or more of these questions, you are prone to anger problems. It's time for a change. If you answered true to 5 questions, you are about average in your angry feelings, but learning some anger management techniques can make you happier.

The Most Important Test. For most men reading this book I suggest that you not spend one second arguing with your wife as to who has the anger problem. One of the purposes of this book is to teach you how never to have an argument with your spouse. Before you get to the section on communication, you can start with a critical practice right now: 1) Find truth in what your wife says. 2) Start your sentence with, "You are right." No "buts"...keep your butt out of the way. 3) Repeat 1 and 2.

Now your wife tells you, "You have a horrible anger problem. You have to read this book, *Anger Busting 101*." The old you might have said, "I have an anger problem? What about you? You are the one who needs to read it." The new you might say, "You are right. I do get angry way too much."

> Please don't use this book to get yourself deeper in the doghouse.

In Summary...

There are many myths about anger that may make it harder for angry men to change their behavior. There also may be a question as to whether you are a real rageaholic. Most men would be glad to find a way to live a happier life and have a happier marriage. There may be some suggestions you can use to achieve those goals. You don't have to decide if you are a rager or how bad of a rager you may be.

In Section I we will address the new ABCs of managing your anger: Abstain, Believe, Communicate. Not all angry men are the same. Section II is designed to help women understand which men can change and which men cannot. It will also help women learn ways to get their man's attention. Section III examines the ABCs for women who are trying to help their men change.

This book is written primarily for angry men and the women who have to suffer them. The principles and techniques discussed in this book can also be applied to make most marriages more rewarding, regardless of the amount of rage in the relationship.

SECTION I:

THE ABCs FOR ANGRY MEN

"I thank God for my handicaps, for through them I have found myself, my work and my God."

—Helen Keller

RUBES®

By Leigh Rubin

By permission of Leigh Rubin and Creators Syndicate, Inc.

Chapter 1

A = *Abstain*

Abstain From These Behaviors

"We have found that justified anger ought to be left to those better qualified to handle it."
—*Twelve Steps and Twelve Traditions*, Alcoholics Anonymous

Introduction

The first question to ask yourself is, "Why am I reading this book?" The fact that you even have this book means that either you realize you have a problem, your wife is leaving you, the children aren't talking to you, you have been fired or are on the verge of being fired, or you are in trouble with the law. Or you may just feel guilty at how your anger is affecting your family and your life. Apart from the damage your anger is doing to your marriage, we know that conflict between parents is traumatic for children. Seligman and Seligman followed the lives of 400 children for five years, focusing on those children whose parents fight and those children whose parents do not fight. They found that children of fighting families are more depressed than children from nonfighting families. Seligman and Seligman noted:

> Once children's parents start fighting, these children become unbridled pessimists....They see bad events as permanent and pervasive....Their workflow has

43

changed from the rosy optimism of childhood to the grim pessimism of a depressed adult. I believe that many children react to their parents' fighting by developing a loss of security so shattering that it marks the beginning of a lifetime of depression.[11]

"What can I do to never blow up at my wife or family again?"

To fully recover, we rageaholics must abstain from certain behaviors. We must stop saying, "I'm not going to just sit there and let her talk to me that way" or "She is the one who needs to shut up for once." You may have made resolutions such as:

"I will never do that again."

"I will never scream like that again."

"I will never put my hands on her again."

Making resolutions like "I will never rage again" doesn't work. If it did, you would not be reading this book.

While our intentions are often good, we rageaholics just can't make our resolutions work. Simple self-talk and global affirmations about our "inherent goodness" don't work. Although we should be aware of our internal voices, we must also learn to develop new voices to replace the "soldier talk" and the heroic rescue fantasies discussed in this chapter. More than anything else, we must have a plan of action. What follows is an effective action plan for what we can do to abstain from expressing anger.

When Angry—Stop the Following 15 Behaviors:

1. Stop speaking.

> *"He who guards his mouth preserves his life; he who opens wide his lips comes to ruin."*
> —Proverbs 13:13

> *"Even a fool who keeps silent is considered wise; when he closes his lips, he is deemed intelligent."*
> —Proverbs 17:28

Stop telling yourself:

"I'm not going to just sit here and let her talk to me that way."

"She's the one who needs to shut up for once."

The all-time, fail-proof, safest action when we feel rage well up inside is silence. We must abstain from speaking, keep the lid on our pressure cooker, keep the valve shut and turn off the fire by stopping the thoughts that build up the steam. We either have to change our internal dialogue or learn to shut it off. One example of silence is illustrated by the following dialogue:

> *One Saturday morning Joe's wife asked him to accompany her on errands, something he hated doing. It was raining, the traffic was bumper to bumper and the one hour of errands had turned into four hours. Debbie, who had been in a car accident only a few months before, was panicking, criticizing and directing Joe's driving. Although Joe was getting angry, he decided to follow the principle of silence on the topic.*

Debbie: "Why aren't you talking to me?"

Joe: "Sweetheart, I'm concentrating on driving."

Debbie: "Are you mad at me?"

Joe: "Not in the least."

Debbie: "Are you sure?"

Joe: "I've never been more in love with you in my life."

Silence is the number one behavior to learn. Being silent doesn't mean that we have stopped listening. Instead, it means that we are in control of our anger.

Silence and Anger Abstinence. When working at the Administration Hospital drug abuse unit, I met a new patient in the hallway. He said, "I understand you help people with their rage problems. I really want to go through this program, but I've never gone for more than three days without blowing up. What should I do?"

Without speaking, I motioned for him to follow me to my office, then to wait at the door. I got a 3x5 card out of the drawer and wrote on it, "WHEN ANGRY, DON'T SPEAK."

Puzzled, he looked at me. "I'm not sure what you mean? When somebody says something that makes me angry, I'm just supposed to say nothing?"

I gestured for him to hand the card back and in parentheses I wrote, "SHUT UP." and then waved good-bye.

The next day the patient came up to me and complained, "I can't take it. I just can't be quiet when someone curses me. I've never been able to take it and I can't imagine I ever will."

"Let me ask you something," I said. "If you were walking down the street one night and someone jumped out from behind a building and stuck a pistol to the side of your head and said, 'If you utter one sound, I'm going to blow your brains out,' do you think you could restrain yourself from speaking in that situation?"

"Well, yeah."

"Do you think you could restrain yourself even if he cursed you and said bad things about your mother and insulted you in all kinds of ways?"

"Yeah, sure."

Then, I explained, "I think it *is* possible to restrain ourselves. It's just that our motivation has not often been strong enough. Instead of saying things like, 'I *can't* stand it,' you can say things that will turn the fire off like, 'I *can* take it.' If your motivation is strong enough, you can practice not speaking. It can be done. I have seen many men do it when their marriages were at stake."

2. Stop staying.

> "Better a patient man than a warrior. A man who controls his temper is better than one who takes a city."
> —Proverbs 16:32

Stop telling yourself:

"But she hates it when I walk out on her."

"It's my house; I'm not going anywhere."

What does "stop staying" mean? It means leave the scene quickly and quietly. Imagine an anger scale of 0 to 10. Zero equals no anger and ten equals rage. Once you have gone to 5 or higher, get out. It's probably too late if you wait until you get to 8 or above. In fact, once you get that angry, you won't be able to restrain yourself from speaking and you probably won't be able to leave. When you feel your anger start to go up the scale or if it just jumps up to 5, don't stay. Leave quietly.

How do you know when you've reached a five on the anger scale? Well, you should begin to monitor your anger signs to become aware of your internal states. Each person has different physical responses when he gets angry. Some people will sweat profusely; others will feel their muscles tightening. Some will get clammy hands, and still others will feel their blood pressure rising. Learn your anger signs.

Several years ago I ran an anger management course for domestic violence offenders. The men were required by the probation department to attend the course. To bring the points home, I used role-playing, with one man playing the wife and the other the husband:

Husband: (enters the room) "Hi, honey, what's for dinner?"

Wife: (exploding into profanity at full volume while standing inches from his face) "You don't deserve for me to cook, you #.$%&.*$%. If you want to eat, cook it yourself. I'm tired of cooking for you."

Husband: "I'm taking a time-out and I'll be back in an hour." (This is a real-life time-out, not the mutually agreed upon one described in most self-help books.)

Wife: (screams) "I won't be here when you get back."

Husband: (He goes out the door and closes it quietly. He returns in one hour—about 30 seconds in the role-play—and tests the waters.) Changing the subject, he says: "Nice weather we're having. How was your day?"

Wife: "Fine until I saw your %.&@$#*# face. What are you doing back here? I told you to stay away."

Husband: At this point, the husband decides to take a Motel 6 time-out and says, "I'll talk to you in the morning."

I explained to the group that the key point here is to stay away until your wife calms down. If she hits and you defend yourself, you can be arrested again.

Take as long and as many time-outs as needed for your wife to calm down. On the other hand, spouses don't like to be left, even during an argument. They will often say something like, "You chicken, come back here and talk to me like a man." (This comment pushed the buttons on most men in the group.) Or, "You're always running out when I want to talk to you."

> When the new patient at the VA came back and asked what to do next, I wrote, "DON'T STAY." To put it bluntly, number one is to "shut up" and number two is to "get out."

3. Stop staring.

Stop telling yourself:

"I was just looking at her."

"I'm not staring. She wants me to look at her when she talks, so I was looking."

Couples who stare intensely at each other when they are angry are actually glaring. Looking someone in the eye in a hostile way is taunting and provocative. On the streets this kind of behavior has led to more than a few severe beatings and even deaths. Glaring is a primitive fight or flight response and is often a precursor to physical violence. Many ragers use staring and the "evil eye" to intimidate those around them.

Richard, Luanda and the kids were sitting around the dinner table discussing the upcoming weekend. The youngest child asked what they were going to do.

Luanda: "Nothing. There's no money this weekend. Your father bought season tickets for the basketball game and we're broke."

Richard: "I've been saving for those season tickets and the money didn't come out of the household budget."

Luanda: "Richard, all of our money is part of the household budget."

Richard stares angrily at Luanda.

Luanda: "Richard, don't give me that 'evil eye.' I'm not afraid of you."

Luanda stares back and Richard becomes angrier. Composing himself, Richard backs off and stares at the floor.

Richard: "Listen, honey, let's have a nice dinner and talk about the money problems later."

Luanda also backs off and Richard's anger outburst is defused. The family continues to have a pleasant dinner.

> Don't stare when you're angry. Look at the floor, look at the ceiling, look anywhere, but don't stare at the other person. It only inflames your anger.

4. Stop interrupting.

Stop telling yourself:

"I have to interrupt because what she is saying is wrong."

"What do you mean don't interrupt her? She was the one who interrupted me."

It is sometimes impossible to tell who is interrupting whom when anger begins to rise. It is important not to interrupt and to allow others to interrupt you, but this is the one thing that most of us ragers feel we can't stand.

Why is it that we ragers always think we are on the verge of making some profound and interesting point when someone interrupts us? We say, "Wait a minute. That's the one thing I can't stand. I'm just about to get to the point here." We need to train ourselves not to interrupt others. If someone interrupts us, we must allow it. If interrupted, we need to go back to number one: Abstain from speaking. If we are getting madder, then we shouldn't stay. Our wives will notice the silence and they will notice us leaving quietly. They will also notice that we are allowing them to interrupt us without interrupting them.

I once had a session with a trial lawyer and his wife. Every time I started talking the attorney would talk over me.

Therapist: "Excuse me, I'm interrupting you."

Lawyer: "But I'm not finished."

Therapist: "You're never finished, which is part of your problem."

Lawyer: (angrily) "Listen, I'm paying you to listen to me and I'm going to finish."

Therapist: (laughing) "No, you don't understand. You are paying me to interrupt you because you want to stay married. This behavior is one of the reasons your wife is throwing you out."

Lawyer: "Okay, go ahead, but I don't like it."

If you have successfully followed the first four behaviors, you are on your way to controlling your addiction to rage and are now ready for the next stage.

> Abstain from interrupting. You will have made a significant change in your behavior if you practice the first four behaviors. Others will notice the difference.

5. Stop cursing.

Stop telling yourself:

"Hey, you don't know where I work. Over there, everybody curses all the time."

"You mean I'm supposed to say 'ouch' instead of *&.%@#$+ when I stub my toe?"

One of the most important behaviors to abstain from immediately is profanity. The reason is not from a moral or religious point of view, but from a psychological and behavioral perspective. If we don't curse, we don't inflame our rage. If we abstain from all profanity, no matter what, it will immediately reduce the amount of anger we must manage. In other words, cursing adds steam to our pressure cooker and inflames our anger.

A few years ago I saw a patient who had recently been arrested on a domestic violence charge. Ralph had gotten into a fight with his 19-year-old stepson, and when his wife tried to break it up, he pushed her. The stepson's girlfriend called the police and Ralph was arrested. His wife filed for divorce and got a restraining order. In the office Ralph sobbed that he would do anything to get his wife back. He wanted to know what he could do today so that she would know he was changing. My answer was, "There's something you can do, but it's difficult."

"I'll do anything," he said.

I replied, "Stop all profanity. Everywhere and all the time."

"You don't understand. I've worked for the railroad for 20 years. How can I stop cursing?" he pleaded.

I asserted, "If you want to get your wife back, you'll be the only railroad employee who doesn't curse."

"I'll do it," he sobbed.

In the next session Ralph reported that he wasn't arguing with his wife over the telephone as intensely as before. He thought it was because he had stopped cursing. In the third session Ralph reported a romantic interlude. He felt things were finally going to work out and he would call if he needed any more therapy.

If you were to have a temper tantrum without profanity, where you stomp your foot and say, "Gee whiz, I'm really upset by that. Golly gee, that really frustrated me," then took a blood sample, there would likely not be any biochemical change. If you were to pretend having a temper tantrum with profanity, even though you were not angry, then took a blood sample, you would find a biochemical change. These changes would occur because the use of profanity for rageaholics starts the adrenaline flowing.

So, if we abstain from profanity, we will have less anger and people will be less angry at us. Some people can do this quickly; for other people, it takes a while to get a handle on it. Some men in anger groups have worked on stopping profanity for an entire year before they went through a full day without cursing. Other men have been able to do it almost instantly.

> Profanity increases the steam in the pressure cooker.
> If we stop cursing, we lower the heat and reduce the
> steam.

6. Stop name-calling.

Stop telling yourself:

"But she was calling me names. She's the one with the problem."

"I didn't mean it when I called her those names. She understands that I was just angry."

Name-calling is another way to produce steam. It is also a behavior that we rageaholics need to abstain from immediately. We need to stop using not only the vile, crude names, but also names like "stupid" and "crazy." Using those names inflames an argument. When we name-call, even in jest, our significant other doesn't know we are "just kidding" and doesn't think it is funny. Name-calling hurts others and it raises our anger level.

Name-calling is a destructive element in a relationship. If you call your wife a bad name, there's no going back. It could take months for her to recover. You may think, "I'm over my anger. Why can't she let it go?" Ragers don't understand the level of destruction caused when they call their partner a name. It's like former President Truman saying to the emperor of Japan, "It was just a couple of bombs. What's the big deal?"

A typical name-calling scenario might go like this. John is relaxing and watching television. Mary, his wife, has taken work home and is busily typing a report on her computer. Suddenly her monitor goes blank. Mary walks into the living room and nicely asks John to look at her computer. After working with computers all day, John is in no mood to troubleshoot computer problems at home. Mary keeps on asking him to see what's wrong with her computer.

Mary: "John, please look at my computer and tell me what's wrong with it."

John: "I'm not in the mood. I'll do it tomorrow."

Mary: "But, John, I need to get this report done for work by tomorrow morning."

John: "It'll have to wait. The NBA playoffs are on."

Mary: "I need it now. It will take only a minute."

John: "Okay, fine. Will you leave me alone then?" (John looks at the computer and finds that the monitor cable has become dislodged from its socket. He puts it back in and the computer works. Irritated at being interrupted, John blurts out, "You know, you're really stupid. Couldn't you figure this out by yourself?")

Mary is silent. Six months later...

John: "Mary, would you help me figure out how to use this new food processor?"

Mary: "I can't help you. Remember, I'm stupid."

John: "Where did that come from?"

Mary: "Don't you remember telling me how stupid I am?"

> Name-calling hurts others and it inflames our anger.

7. Stop threatening.

Stop telling yourself:

"Sometimes I just want to warn her she's about to go too far."

"You are not going to talk to me that way. No one is going to talk to me that way. I don't take that kind of talk from anyone."

Those are threats that imply, "I will leave you or hurt you." Even subtle threats wreak havoc in terms of your partner's fear of abandonment. A typical dialogue that avoids threats might look something like this:

Justin returns home late after working at the refinery plant. Before coming home he stops at the tavern for a couple of beers. Heather, his girlfriend, is upset because he didn't phone.

Justin: "Hi, Honey, I'm home."

Heather: "Where have you been?"

Justin:	"I was working late and then stopped off for a few beers."
Heather:	"Right, you were working late and stopped for beers. Are you seeing her again?"
Justin:	"Who?"
Heather:	"Your girlfriend."
Justin:	"What girlfriend? I don't have a girlfriend. I'm not seeing anybody but you. I've never dated anyone since we got together."
Heather:	"I don't believe you."
Justin:	"Honey, I really love you and I am sorry you don't trust me. I know it must be hard for you to have these suspicions. What can I do to help?"

Some women may find Justin's last statement patronizing and be suspicious of whether Justin means it. I would say to Justin, "Say it and *mean it*." If she doubts you, then convince her. This is no time for sarcasm.

The object is to make Heather feel more secure through the use of reassurance rather than argument, accusations or threats, which would only increase her anger and fear of abandonment.

Justin is thinking: "I can't take the accusations and suspicions anymore. It's driving me nuts. I need to get out of this relationship. If she doesn't trust me, I'll leave. Maybe then I'll find someone who will trust me." Instead of using threats, Justin remembers the behaviors for controlling his anger.

Justin:	"Honey, I love you a lot and I'm sorry you don't trust me. I know it must be hard for you to have these suspicions. I will never see another woman and will never leave you, no matter what."

Heather feels more secure and calms down. Had Justin used threats, Heather's insecurity, anger and fear of abandonment would have been increased.

> We need to monitor ourselves. We need to stop using threats and implied threats.

8. Stop pointing.

Furthermore, stop telling yourself:

"I was just trying to get her attention."

"I am not aware of my pointing—it's a natural thing to do."

Pointing a finger at someone is frequently an unconscious behavior. We ragers might need to ask our spouse and friends to tell us when we are doing this. In my therapy groups, members make each other aware of finger-pointing. Instead of pointing, you need to look at yourself rather than point at the other person. (It is physically true that when you point a finger, one finger is pointing out while three other fingers are pointing back at you.)

> Identify pointing as soon as it starts. When a client pulls his hand up from his lap to point, I say, "No pointing." Often, he'll put that hand down and then pick up the other. Again, I say, "No pointing."

9. Stop yelling, raising your voice, or talking in a mean tone.

Stop telling yourself:

"Yelling is the only way to get her attention and let her know I'm serious."

"I'm not yelling. She's not listening. If she would just listen, I wouldn't have to yell."

Like other self-destructive behaviors, raising our voices and yelling only fuels our anger. Like finger-pointing, we are sometimes unaware of how loud we are talking. First, we must gain some awareness of these behaviors. On a scale of 0-10 (0 equals silence), when you raise your voice to a 2 or 3, it needs to be brought to your attention. (How do you know if it's a 2 or a 3? Ask other people to let you know.) It is important for spouses, family members, friends and therapists to intervene early when we begin to raise our voices. They can say something like, "You are beginning to raise your voice. Please lower it." As a rager, our appropriate response should be, "You are right. Thanks for pointing it out." Having others point out to us when we are raising our voice and yelling will help us monitor our behavior.

Phil and Nancy are sitting around the kitchen table discussing how to pay their bills. Phil is becoming increasingly upset as it becomes clearer that they will not be able to pay their bills this month without borrowing money. The conversation goes like this:

Phil: "I'm worried. I don't know how we can pay the bills this month."

Nancy: "We'll manage somehow."

Phil: "What do you mean we'll manage somehow? We don't have the money. If you didn't waste so much money on clothes, we'd be doing fine."

Nancy: "Stop yelling at me."

Phil: "If you'd just listen, I wouldn't have to yell."

Phil: (composing himself) "You're right. Thanks for pointing out that I was yelling."

> What should rageaholics do when others point out that we are yelling? We should thank our partner or therapist for telling us when we are raising our voice since this can be an unconscious mechanism outside of the awareness of rageaholics beginning the recovery process.

Furthermore, stop telling yourself:

"Hey, what is she talking about? I wasn't yelling, cursing or anything."

"This is how I normally talk. If she wanted some mushy-mouth guy, she should have married one. That ain't me."

The "mean tone" is an important but hard issue for rageaholics to understand. I often tell angry men that when they come for therapy, they think they've signed up for a quarter-mile race. They run the quarter mile, sprint the last few feet, and throw up their arms in victory, only to be told by the referee that this is a mile race. They have three more laps to run. What am I talking about?

Many men work very hard for several months to contain their yelling and cursing, yet their wives will say something like, "You're no better than you ever were." I warn men about this when they start. By itself, stopping angry behaviors is not enough. It's necessary, but not sufficient, to have a happy marriage. And it's definitely not sufficient if your wife is teetering on the edge of divorce. After a few months the wife will come into a therapy session to talk about how things are going:

> **Wife:** "He's no better than he was."
>
> **Husband:** "Sweetheart, I've gone three months without profanity, without name-calling, without blowing up and without raising my voice. I haven't thrown things. I haven't touched you in anger. I haven't slammed the door. What are you talking about?"
>
> **Therapist:** "I will give you credit. I acknowledge you for these things because I am your therapist and I know you have changed and I know this has been hard work, but there are still things that your wife feels very hurt about that may be very difficult for you to understand."
>
> **Wife:** "He still talks to me in a mean tone and that hurts me so much."
>
> **Husband:** "A mean tone, a mean voice? I don't know what you're talking about."

Wives can point out to us when they hear a mean tone. Even though we are abstaining from the more obvious behaviors of rage like touching or slamming doors, our wives may feel that we despise or hate them, just by the tone of our voice. Although this is a difficult concept for rageful men to understand, it is very important. It starts what I call the other three laps to a happy marriage. I will examine the opposite of "mean tones" when we discuss communication later in this book. At this point, it is important that we become aware of any time we use a mean tone, a stern tone or a harsh tone.

> Disgust, disdain and hatred can be communicated by tone of voice.

10. Stop being sarcastic. Stop mocking.

Stop telling yourself:

"She doesn't understand that I'm just joking."

"She has no sense of humor. That's the real problem."

Sarcastic one-liners are fine for television sitcoms, but they don't work for maintaining a real-life marriage or a happy family life. When the actors leave the stage after delivering their sarcastic remark, they go back to their dressing rooms. After we drop a sarcastic one-liner, we have to stick around for the consequences. Often ragers don't realize how much pain and hurt our sarcastic remarks cause. We misjudge the impact of our sarcasm. We need to stop making wisecracks about our wife and family members.

While visiting her parents, Janet (a compulsive spender) received a gift from her grandmother. It was a beautiful necklace that had been owned by her great-grandmother. To show her appreciation, Janet called her grandmother to thank her.

In the past, Janet had taken gifts of jewelry and pawned them to help pay her bills. As the whole family sat around admiring the necklace, her father commented, "I bet as soon as you finish this dinner, you'll be burnin' rubber to get to the nearest pawn shop." Everyone at the table laughed, including Janet's husband and mother.

Angrily, Janet rose from the table and left her father's house. In fact, she was so angry she didn't return for a year.

> Sarcasm is a way of expressing our anger and humiliating others.

In addition, stop telling yourself:

"I was just trying to show her what it sounds like when she snivels about work all the time."

"That's just the way I let her know when she's nagging me too much."

Having a long-standing problem with anger, Robert was overly jealous of his wife. He constantly fantasized that she was flirting with almost every man she saw. Robert was particularly upset when he thought Rachel was flirting with men over the telephone. Before going home from work, he called to talk to Rachel. The line was busy and Rachel didn't answer call waiting. Robert grew more angry and jealous as he drove back home.

Robert: "I'm home."

Rachel: "Hi, honey. How was your day?"

Robert: "Who were you talking to on the phone?"

Rachel: "Just a friend."

Robert: "Why didn't you pick up when you heard the call waiting? Were you screening calls?"

Rachel: (laughing) "Why? Are you jealous? I was only talking to Mindy."

Robert: (mocking Rachel's laugh) "Tee hee hee, I was only talking to Mindeee."

Robert's mocking made Rachel feel humiliated, put down and ashamed.

> Mocking is one of the cruelest behaviors. Like sarcasm, being mocked by someone we care about is very painful.

11. Stop throwing things, slamming doors, or banging walls.

Stop telling yourself:

"It's just a way to let off steam. Besides, I'm not hurting anyone."

"At least I don't break things like I used to. Now I usually just throw pillows."

We need to stop throwing things like pillows, keys and other objects. All objects including shirts, jackets and underwear should also not be thrown. Throwing is an aggressive act that is perceived as threatening and intimidating by those around us. Throwing things—regardless of how harmless the objects are—fuels our anger.

> Don't throw anything in anger.

Also stop telling yourself:

"Slamming doors is just my way of letting her know I really want to be left alone."

"I don't see who or what it hurts to release my anger a little."

Slamming a door shut is the ultimate "last word." We ragers were trained in the "two slam exit method." First, we curse out whomever is in the room, then slam the door. We wait a few seconds, then open the door again, say a few more vile things, and slam it shut. This action results in several things. First, it fuels our anger. Secondly, it is a provocative act that reeks of intimidation. Thirdly, it says that we won't stick around to work things out. Slamming doors is also a good way to infuriate our partner or family member.

Jason had a long-standing anger problem and learned early the "value" of slamming doors. A recent fight with his wife, Marlene, over who was responsible for washing the dishes that night resulted in a fiery outburst.

Jason: "I'm not doing the dishes tonight."

Marlene: "Yes, you are. It's your turn."

Jason: "I'm not doing them. Period."

Marlene: "Then you won't be eating supper here tomorrow night."

Jason: (heading for the door) "You know, Marlene, you are acting like a real baby. I've had it with your stupid childish behavior." Jason walks out and slams the door. A few seconds later he walks back into the room and yells, "You are the ultimate self-centered princess just like your mother." He walks out again, slamming the door behind him.

Marlene: Finding his behavior too much to bear, she follows Jason into the driveway yelling, "Don't come back, you lazy, no-good jerk." Marlene's timing is perfect as the neighbors are milling around just in time to hear her yelling.

Jason: At the next counseling session Jason says, "I don't know what's wrong with Marlene. She followed me into the driveway yelling and embarrassed me in front of our neighbors. Marlene is really the one with the anger problem."

> Slamming doors keeps our anger going. It fans the flames. It often pushes others "over the edge" with their anger.

12. Stop all non-affectionate touching.

Stop telling yourself:

"She was out of control. I was just holding her on the bed so she could get control of herself."

"I was just defending myself when she tried to slap me."

It's unacceptable to touch in anger, including any kind of aggressive touching like pushing or holding. It's also a bad idea. If the police are called and your spouse or girlfriend has bruises, that is domestic violence. In that instance, you can be arrested and jailed.

Ed and Carol got into a fight when she found out he was having an affair with a co-worker. During the screaming and yelling match, Carol became overwrought with emotion and hit Ed. According to Ed, he held her down on the bed to help her regain control. When the neighbors called the police, the following dialogue ensued:

Police officer: "What's going on here?"

Carol: "He attacked me."

Ed: "That's not true. I held her down on the bed so that she could regain her composure. I was just trying to help her."

Carol: "Look at how he bruised me. Look at my black and blue arms. Is this helping me?"

After looking at the bruises on Carol's arm, the police officer arrested Ed on charges of domestic violence. He was not moved by Ed's attempt to "help" Carol. Ed broke the law by physically restraining his wife.

> Don't touch, hold or push a spouse or family member in anger. Aggressive touching is a crime and men will be jailed for committing it.

13. Stop telling "hero stories."

Stop telling yourself:

"I just wanted you to understand what really happened."

"I did pretty good considering I was provoked."

"Hero stories" are stories we tell about how we lost our temper or made a sarcastic remark. When we retell the story, it makes us look like a hero for standing up against someone. Seldom do we tell these stories with shame; mostly we tell them with pride. It's as if we are waiting for our audience to say, "What a man" or "Yeah, you really told her off." Often we find ourselves using profanity when telling and retelling the story. Telling hero stories is like getting two rushes for the price of one. We lose our temper and get a rush of adrenaline, then we call and tell a friend our hero story and get another rush.

I was running an anger group at the Veterans Administration hospital when a patient came in on Monday after a weekend pass. Larry started screaming and cursing about how he was going to kill his wife. As it turned out, his wife had left him for another man. He began describing to the group what he had told her on the phone he would do to them.

It was a hero story about how bad he was, how tough he was and how afraid of him they were. I told Larry to put his elbows on his knees, drop his gaze and talk about how he really felt. After a brief silence, Larry broke down and started sobbing about how hurt he was and how he was dying inside. Behind the hero story was not a warrior, but a man in great pain and anguish over the loss of a loved one.

Hero stories only fuel our anger by making us look bigger than we really are. They often hide pain, anguish and fear.

> When I am working with a man in one of my angry men's groups, I will sometimes say, "I need to interrupt you because this is sounding like a hero story. Rather than tell us what your wife and son did that led up to your anger slip, just tell us what you did wrong and, more importantly, what you could have done differently."

14. Stop sighing, clucking, or rolling your eyes.

Stop telling yourself:

"Well, it's discouraging to hear her complain all the time."

"My sighs just mean I'm tired. It wasn't directed at her. She's too touchy."

Another behavior to abstain from is using various kinds of sighs. These sounds are often a way to express anger, disgust or disapproval. The sighs can also heat up an argument, especially if people are overly sensitive to each other's moods.

Missy: "Let's go to a movie tonight. I really need to get out of the house."

Carl: (sighing) "What do you want to see?"

Missy: "You never want to go anywhere. All you want to do is sit at home and watch television."

Carl: "I said I would go to the movies. What's the problem?"

Missy: "Your sigh tells me that you don't really want to go. You are just doing this to appease me. I don't want to drag you anywhere. I'll just go by myself."

Carl: "I'm not sighing because I don't want to go to the movies but because I'm tired."

Missy: "Yeah, right."

> Sighs can be easily mistaken by another person as an expression of negative feelings. They can also be a way to express anger.

If you have teenagers in your home, you are familiar with clucking and "tssking." (Clucking and "tssking" are special nonverbal techniques that teenagers use to drive their parents over the edge.) A typical conversation might go like this:

Parent: "Will you please take out the trash?"

Teenager: "Tssk."

Parent: "What did you say?"

Teenager: "Nothing."

Parent: "Don't make those sounds to me."

Teenager: "What sounds? Why are you getting so upset? I didn't say anything."

These nonverbal explosive responses generate a lot of hostility in marriages. More and more researchers are finding that couples express most of the hostility to each other in nonverbal ways, so the *how* is as important as the *what* that we say.

> Nonverbal responses like clucking fuel anger in ourselves and our spouse. They should be recognized, avoided and stopped.

Rolling your eyes can intensify or even start an argument. For example, David and Leah invited a couple to their home for a dinner party. During the dinner conversation Leah talked in detail about their last trip to France, forgetting that she had talked to the couple about it before. Fearing that the guests would be bored, David rolled his eyes when she announced that she would get the photo album. When the guests left, David asked Leah if she had a good time.

Leah: "No. I was miserable."

David: "Why?"

Leah: "You embarrassed and humiliated me."

David: "How?"

Leah: "You don't know? You don't remember rolling your eyes when I said I'd get the photo album?"

David: "Honey, I was only kidding."

Leah: "Kid with someone else. Don't joke at my expense. Don't ever again humiliate and embarrass me like that in front of people."

> We can communicate disgust and anger nonverbally by rolling our eyes.

15. Stop criticizing and stop lecturing.

Stop telling yourself:

"If I don't criticize her, how will she know when she does something wrong?"

"You mean I can't express any of my feelings?"

It is essential that we abstain from criticism. A lot of men with rage problems think our job is to help our wives improve by pointing out their shortcomings. Stopping this behavior in ourselves calls for a dramatic shift in values, something we will discuss later in this book.

Jack and Suzanne have been married for 10 years and have experienced marital conflict for most of that time. Suzanne is fed up with the marriage and has demanded that Jack join her in marital therapy. During the third session, the dialogue went like this:

Suzanne: "I'm tired of Jack criticizing me."

Therapist: "What do you mean? Give me an example."

Suzanne: "Last night I was cutting up cabbage for dinner. Jack walked to the kitchen counter and criticized the way I was doing it. He told me I should be cutting it differently."

Therapist: "Jack, would you give up criticizing her cabbage cutting in order to save the marriage?"

Jack: "I was just trying to help her. Isn't it my job to help her become a better cook?"

Therapist: "It's not your job to help her with anything she doesn't specifically ask for help with. If Suzanne wanted your help to become a better cook, she'd ask for it. Jack, I know you think criticism expresses your love and concern, but Suzanne doesn't see it as concern, only criticism."

> It is not our job in life to point out what others are doing wrong.

Driving

This chapter has focused on controlling our anger in family relationships, but what we do in our family lives and what we do in the outside world are interconnected. Because of this, we must abstain from anger in our everyday lives as well. This includes activities like driving, where road rage is a reflection of our anger. It means practicing *recovery driving*.

Once I ran a course for men on probation for domestic violence. At the first meeting I announced, "I have the secret that will keep you out of jail for domestic violence while this course is going on."

"What?" they asked.

"Change the way you drive."

In unison they responded, "What?" "No way." "That's crazy." "Whaddya mean?"

"You can't expect to abstain from expressing anger when you get home if you drive all the way there with one hand on the horn and the other out the window with your middle finger up," I stated matter-of-factly.

I have often heard men in my office say that they will do anything to stop the divorce and get back into the house. When they ask what they can do today, my answer is, "Change the way you drive back to the office. That can be the first tangible evidence that you can change."

What are the guidelines for *recovery driving*?
1. Drive within 5 m.p.h. of the speed limit.
2. If you drive more than 5 m.p.h. over the speed limit, then drive under the speed limit for the next 10 minutes.
3. No honking of the horn in anger.
4. Once the other driver sees you, stop honking.
5. Stop on yellow lights.
6. If someone wants to get in front of you, let him or her in and smile. Avoid eye contact when another driver is angry at you.
7. Make no critical comments about anyone else's driving.

In Summary...

Following the simple abstinence techniques described in this chapter is difficult and often painful at first. When men come for therapy, I tell them that depressed women often find therapy very relieving. For angry men, however, abstaining from anger during the first few months is difficult and painful. However, the simple technique of abstinence is effective in stopping anger and rage outbursts. It will also reduce the amount of anger you feel. The rewards that will come in your relationships and in your work life will make it worth the effort.

ABSTAIN FROM THESE BEHAVIORS WHEN YOU ARE ANGRY.

1. Stop speaking when angry.
2. Stop staying when angry.
3. Stop staring when angry.
4. Stop interrupting—no matter what.
5. Stop cursing—completely stop, no matter what.
6. Stop name-calling, no matter what.
7. Stop threatening.
8. Stop pointing.
9. Stop yelling, raising your voice, or talking in a mean tone.
10. Stop being sarcastic. Stop mocking.
11. Stop throwing things, slamming doors, or banging walls.
12. Stop all non-affectionate touching.
13. Stop telling "hero stories."
14. Stop sighing, clucking, or rolling your eyes.
15. Stop criticizing. Stop lecturing.

As an added measure,

16. Stop speeding.

CHAPTER 2

B = BELIEVE

BELIEVE IN THESE PRINCIPLES FOR PEACE, HAPPINESS AND PERMANENT CHANGE

Stop telling yourself:

"I've told you 'I love you.' Isn't that good enough?"

"I've stopped raging. Isn't that good enough?"

Congratulations to those of you who have stopped raging. That may be good enough and that may be all you need to do. Some men, however, find that they can abstain for a while, but then they are back to their old behaviors. Some of you may find that abstaining from the 15 behaviors outlined in Part I is enough to get you back into your house or to get the divorce put on hold. It may have been enough for you to complete the Anger Management Class and now you can get off probation.

However, many of you may want more than that. You may want a happy marriage or you may even want to find a deeper level of happiness than you ever dreamed possible.

> Some men end up being grateful for the crisis that brought them to this book because the way they had been living their lives had not been working anyway.

This section invites you to look inside yourself and examine the values by which you have lived your life up to now. A shift in values will allow you to maintain the changes you have already made without all the effort you may now be exerting. The following 20 principles, if practiced, will prevent all but the mildest irritation from arising.

We began with abstaining, which can bring rapid change from the outside in. Believing in a new set of principles will be working from the inside out and can sustain the changes you have made. We, as men, were raised with principles or values that can work against us in creating a happy life and particularly a happy marriage. Many of the principles we operate from keep us from having a sense of peace, enjoyment and pleasure in the world. In this chapter we will discuss some of the universal spiritual principles common to all major spiritual and religious traditions and how they may specifically apply to men with rage problems.

Let's talk about different values on which you can base your behavior that will lead to a happier marriage, happiness in your work and more peace inside.

The only thing you will need to know about God to practice these spiritual principles is that "You ain't Him." These principles can be understood and applied by atheists, agnostics or people of any religion. In order to make room for these changes, we rageful men must realize that we do not control the universe.

To understand that we are not supposed to be running the show is a big step forward and a profound spiritual shift that is easier said than done. While we may talk spiritual values, most of the angry behavior is based on the principle of "My wife, the kids, other drivers and co-workers should do it the right way (my way)." The world was not set up for any of us to have our way. Of course, we don't want our wife to have an affair. We don't want our children to be on drugs. We don't want to lose our job. We don't want our mother to have Alzheimer's disease. We may have some influence over some of these events, but we don't have absolute influence over much of anything. This underlying concept of resigning as the ruler of the universe is basic to the principles that follow.

For over 60 years Alcoholics Anonymous groups have advocated the use of spiritual principles to overcome addiction and character defects. The book entitled *Alcoholics Anonymous,* originally published in 1939, accepts spirituality as foundational for change: "That was great news to us, for we had assumed we could not make use of spiritual principles unless we accepted many things on faith which seemed difficult to believe. When people presented us with spiritual approaches, how frequently did we say, 'I wish I had what that man has. I'm sure it would work if I could only believe as he believes. But I cannot accept as surely true the many articles of faith which are so plain to him.' So it was comforting to learn that we could commence at a simpler level."[12]

This book is designed as a friendly interfaith resource which does not compete or conflict with your religious views; rather it can enrich and enliven your beliefs and help you apply them even more effectively in your everyday life. Bo Lozoff, who has spent a lifetime of service helping prison inmates apply universal spiritual principles to their lives, has written a book called *Deep and Simple: A Spiritual Path for Modern Times.* He summarizes the great religious traditions:

> I have great affection for the world's religious scriptures, and I believe with all my heart that they show more similarities than differences. None of them would find fault with a lifestyle of simplicity, service and practice. None would find fault with the term *"deep and simple."* According to the world's great scriptures, the meaning of life is deep and the rules of life are simple. An interfaith way to say it is: Everything counts, so be kind. Everything counts—a reminder to the intellect that life is deeper than it may seem; be kind—a simple instruction for the heart. You can't be a good Christian or Muslim or Hindu or Buddhist or Jew or a good anything else until you understand such universal truths as these.[13]

1. Practice self-restraint—don't always express yourself.

The most important principle for angry men to adopt is self-restraint. You are already practicing this principle if you are abstaining from the 15 key behaviors described in Chapter One.

Over the past 50 years, a popular psychological belief advocated expressing your anger and "getting it out." The belief in the value of expressing our feelings has become an almost sacred principle in psychology. However, no major religious or spiritual tradition of the last two thousand years has suggested "getting it all out." Quite to the contrary, the traditional spiritual concept of all religions is restraint. It is a critical concept for rageful men and its importance is summarized below:

> Our first objective will be the development of self-restraint. This carries a top priority rating. When we speak or act hastily or rashly, the ability to be fair minded and tolerant evaporates on the spot. One unkind tirade or one willful snap judgment can ruin our relationship with another person for a whole day or maybe a whole year. Nothing pays off like restraint of tongue and pen. We must avoid quick-tempered criticism and furious power-driven arguments. The same goes for sulking or silent scorn. These are emotional booby traps baited with pride and vengefulness. Our first job is to sidestep the traps. When we are tempted by the bait, we should train ourselves to step back and think. For we can neither think nor act to good purpose until self-restraint has become automatic.[14]

Notice that it says that when we speak or act hastily or rashly it changes our ability to think. Our behavior changes our thinking. Don't get your anger out. Practice self-restraint instead.

> We started this journey by restraining from talking when angry. For some of us, shutting up is a spiritual act. It is acting on the principle of self-restraint. It may require courage to stand our ground quietly and still practice self-restraint. This is the first principle on our new path. So if you are angry, contain it, repress it, stuff it. Whatever words you prefer to use to describe it, practice self-restraint.

You will hear a lot on TV and in self-help books about not bottling up feelings and how we need to let them out. That may be fine for others, but not for us ragers. Our first objective is the development of self-restraint.

2. Practice kindness—not revenge.

> *"Kindness, I've discovered, is everything."*
> —Isaac Bashevis Singer

Stop telling yourself:

"What do you want me to do? Wimp out?"

"I ain't taking that from nobody."

To act in a kind way may require behaving the *opposite of how we feel* when angry or irritated. Some people say it is more important that our behavior and feelings match than that we behave kindly. But to behave in a kind way and to talk with a soft, kind tone is practicing or applying a very important principle: kindness. How does this fit with telling the truth about how we really feel—in other words, "being honest?" Those of us with anger and rage problems have often severely abused the concept of honesty by using it as a club and a weapon to bring pain to those we know and love.

Typically, those of us who have developed rage and violence problems find it easy to tell people what we don't like. There is a higher principle for those of us with rage problems when faced with a dilemma of telling the truth about our feelings versus being kind, gentle and loving. Practice being kind, gentle and loving first. Too many of us ragers have a compulsion to tell others about our anger. Don't.

At least for now, for those of us with a history of rage or violence, we must loosen our grip on telling the truth about how we feel. This does not give us license to lie about everything, just to act on a higher principle when angry. We may be chastised for not telling the truth about our feelings when we are angry, irritated or annoyed, but we must put our recovery first.

When angry it is time to practice a higher principle of kindness by telling a "deeper truth." The deeper truth is that we are hurt, frightened, ashamed or guilty. By using these words, we tell a deeper truth about how we are really feeling. That may not be what is on the surface, but it is what underlies the anger. We can learn more about these deeper feelings and get these words into our vocabulary by saying them, *especially* when we do not feel them.

Deepak Chopra, a western-trained physician from India, says that we can tell we are making progress spiritually in our marriage or close relationships when we practice behavior that feels unnatural, awkward or even embarrassing. Practicing saying words such as hurt, embarrassed, ashamed or anything other than the "A" word (anger) will likely feel awkward at first. Most men have not grown up hearing their fathers say, "I was wrong. I feel helpless. I feel hurt. I feel embarrassed. I feel ashamed." So if you feel unnatural, awkward or even embarrassed, that is an excellent sign you are making progress. You are trying something new.

3. Practice being gracious—not critical.

"Argument and fault finding are to be avoided like the plague."
—Alcoholics Anonymous[15]

Stop telling yourself:

"But what if she's wrong?"

"It's my responsibility to point out what is wrong to my kids."

Most of us with anger and rage problems are attracted to anger and fault-finding like they are drugs we can't live without. Many of us ragers have the underlying belief that it is our job to point out the faults of others, especially our spouse and our children. We believe this to be part of our responsibility as a good father or a good husband.

We need to ask ourselves how much they have changed because of our criticism. Usually criticism of our wives and children only changes how they feel about us, not their behavior. We may have a moral duty to point out the wrongs of our children, but most of us have overdone that. You may want to check with your wife to get her opinion on whether she and the kids could make it if you were to give up criticizing them for a day or maybe a week.

Certainly, with grown children, we could try to get through an entire conversation without offering unsolicited advice or criticism. Ask their help in pointing it out. Agree with them when they do point it out. My 30-year-old daughter and I were making a salad together in the kitchen when I noticed that she was very quiet. I realized I had been giving what I thought were some helpful suggestions. I said, "I guess I have been overdoing the unsolicited advice."

"No kidding," she answered.

We must immediately resign from our job of pointing out what is wrong with our wives. In fact, I often ask clients to write a resignation letter to God stating that they will no longer point out what is wrong with their spouse, their teenage children or freeway drivers.

One colleague suggests that his clients not give any unsolicited advice to any children over 13 years of age. Set limits? Yes. Have consequences? Yes. But no advice. You may want to practice the opposite of fault-finding—giving compliments, gratitude and praise. Focus on practicing the opposite of argument...agreement.

> Your wife may not appreciate your self-restraint because she will not know when you are restraining yourself. However, she will notice your gratitude, compliments and praise. The good news is that you don't have to be creative or original with compliments. You can say these three every day, "I'm glad I married you. You are a beautiful woman. I am a lucky man." It is alright not to be original.

Say a simple "thank you" at every opportunity. The only prayer that one teacher says we need is, "Thank you." We could say those words non-stop as a prayer for the rest of our lives. A good start would be to say them over and over to your wife for the rest of her life.

4. Practice self-examination—not blame.

> *"Putting out of our minds the wrong others have done, we resolutely look for our own mistakes. Where had we been selfish, dishonest, self-seeking and frightened? Though the situation had not been entirely our fault, we tried to disregard the other person involved entirely. Where were we to blame?...We admitted our wrongs honestly and were willing to set these matters straight."*
>
> —Alcoholics Anonymous[16]

Stop telling yourself:

"But she's the one who is wrong."

"She's trying to push my buttons."

What action do you take to get the focus off yourself when you are angry? When someone points out that you are wrong and you feel your anger gauge start to rise, what do you say? The action to take is to speak three simple words that are guaranteed to stop any argument. Some men have never spoken these simple words: "You are right." Keep the focus on your own wrong instead of pointing out where the other person was wrong.

You can change the direction of any discussion by saying: "You were right. I was wrong." You don't have to *know* where you were wrong when you say it. You certainly don't have to *feel* that you were wrong. Say it first, then figure out the one percent you contributed to the problem. This is a good time and place to install an alarm in your head so that when you hear yourself saying, "Yes, but..." sirens and bells go off. "Yes, but..." is always the beginning of an argument.

The way to practice this principle is to say:

    1) "You are right."

    2) "I was wrong."

    3) "I should have..."

4) Then be quiet. Don't say anything. Shut up.

5) Repeat 1-4.

5. Practice empathy—not selfishness.

> *"You must give something to your fellow men. Even if it is a little thing, do something for those who have need of help, something for which you get no pay but the privilege of giving. For remember, you do not live in a world of your own. Your brothers and sisters are here, too."*
>
> —Albert Schweitzer

Stop telling yourself:

"Hey, if I don't look out for Number One, who will?"

"I ain't into sainthood—I just wanna drink a cold beer and watch TV in peace. Is there anything wrong with that?"

The principle of empathy speaks to the root cause of our problem as angry men. What is the root of our problem? Selfishness. Anger occurs when we do not get our way or get what we want. Focusing on ourself to the exclusion of our significant other is a symptom of selfishness. Alcoholics Anonymous identifies this self-preoccupation as central to the addictive process: "Selfishness—self-centeredness! That, we think, is the root of our troubles."[17] How can we practice selflessness in marriage? We can listen to our wife's needs and wants without criticizing her in any way and empathize with how she is thinking or feeling. The phrases we need to practice are:

"What I hear you saying is...Is that right?" *(Then wait in silence.)*

"I see how you could feel that way." *(Then wait in silence.)*

"It must be difficult." *(Then wait in silence; no opinion, no thoughts, no feelings of your own.)*

> Giving up selfishness does not mean doing everything the other person wants you to do. It does mean listening to your wife's wants, needs, ideas and feelings and acknowledging their legitimacy. To be able to take your focus off what you want, what you think, or what you feel for 5 minutes or even 30 seconds is a beginning.

These are some specific ways which give meaning to selflessness in marriage. Pay attention to what she wants, needs, feels and thinks without criticizing, evaluating or judging.

6. Practice surrendering—not dominating.

Stop telling yourself:

"It's my way or the highway."

"I'm tired of being walked on—this time she has pushed me too far."

No major spiritual tradition suggests that the basis of life is to have what you want. A universal expression of all traditions might be, "Any life run on self-will can hardly be a success."[18] Now what is meant by success? Love, peace, happiness and serenity—all of these qualities are achieved as by-products of working for a larger purpose, not trying to arrange life to suit ourselves.

> Our desires arise quicker than our ability to satisfy them, and are often contradictory.

Some of the time you can "let go" of what you want. Anything that angry men have let go of usually has claw marks on it, so you may want to hold your opinions more loosely by saying, "You could be right."

7. Practice service to others—not self-interest.

Stop telling yourself:

"I ain't kissing nobody's rear end."

"I have enough to do at my job."

The principle of service is central to spiritual traditions: "As you did it to one of the least of your brethren, you did it to me," said Jesus.[19] Trying to have our way, which has been the main goal for most of our lives, has led to a life of misery in our closest relationships. Giving up self-centeredness is a radical step for most of us. Happiness is a by-product of living our lives on the principle of service.

Service means giving fully to another person in some way. This means taking the attention off of ourselves by making sure we understand what our wife is saying by repeating it back. "What I hear you saying is...Is that right?" It is a concept we can extend to our spouse by seeing what we can do to make her life easier or better.

8. Practice disciplining yourself—not, "I have to have my way."

Stop telling yourself:

"I don't want to be disciplined. I want to be happy."

"What is she going to do? Whatever she feels like?"

The principle of discipline suggests that leading a principled life requires a fair amount of work. Bo Lozoff has devoted 25 years to bringing the message to prisoners that a happy life can be lived on spiritual principles anywhere you are, especially in prison. "Self-respect requires self-discipline. Decency requires conscience and courage. Kindness requires patience and forgiveness. A good life happens to be a fair amount of work. It is not for the lazy."[20]

> Many people think that making a transition from a self-centered life to one based on principle is going to be full of joy and that the work is going to be easy. It is a journey that requires action, discipline and restraint. It means we are going to practice accepting not getting our way all the time.

9. Practice being patient—not impulsive.

Stop telling yourself:

"When do I get *my* way?"

"I ain't sitting around. I'm going for the gusto, man."

Patience is an important spiritual principle for the rageful or violent man. A lot of our anger is fueled by a sense of "time urgency." Angry men chronically feel that they are late or behind. They have to hurry to make up for lost time.

For example, as I mentioned earlier, angry men often drive with one hand on the horn and their middle finger out the window. Rageful drivers are the most upset when they are cut off in traffic. This experience only happens when you want to go faster than the person who came into the lane. If you drive no more than five miles an hour over the speed limit in the slow lane, you will seldom have the experience of being cut off. If you curb the sense of time urgency, you help minimize the reason to be angry.

If you want to change the way you relate to your wife, start right now by practicing *recovery driving*. The patience that comes with the discipline of driving five miles an hour under the speed limit permeates other areas of your life. For instance, if for the next year you let any driver in front of you who wants to be there, your relationship with your wife will automatically improve.

Many angry men have asked me with tears streaming down their cheeks, "What can I do to get my wife back? I will do anything. Is there something I can do today?"

I say, "Yes. This may not make sense, but change the way you drive back to work from this appointment. If you can change the way you drive, you will begin to change the way you think and feel." Developing patient behavior means driving slower.

I typically start my marital counseling sessions with the question, "What is better this week?" One couples' therapy session went like this:

Therapist: "What is better?"

Rose: "A lot."

Therapist: "Really? Like what?"

Rose: "Just lots of things."

Therapist: "Like what? Give me one example small or large of anything better."

Rose: "Well, like we agreed in the last session, Brian and I were going to have a date on Saturday night.

Well, just about everything went wrong. It was my fault for running late and we missed the movie. But Brian kept saying that it was okay, not to worry. He usually screams and hollers if I am one second late to anything."

Therapist: "Brian, how did you do that?"

Brian: "Do what? You mean not get upset?"

Therapist: "Yeah, Rose says that is a major change for you."

Brian: "Well, I realized that I was making us both miserable and we hadn't had a pleasant night out in several years. Of course, the fact that if I don't change my ways I may never have a chance to go out and have a good time with her, kind of woke me up."

Therapist: "Wow. This is a miracle. Wouldn't you agree, Rose?"

Rose: "Yes, either a miracle or a 'class A con job.' But to tell you the truth, it doesn't make any difference to me because I really had a good time for the first time in years."

> Working on developing patience also means being willing to repeat yourself in a pleasant voice two, three, or four times when your wife is asking you a question from the other room.

10. Practice forgiveness—not punishment.

Stop telling yourself:

"When was the last time she forgave me? Never, that's when."

"Why should I forgive her?"

Sometimes other people do wrong us. Sometimes we are wronged and we want revenge. We want to pay them back by telling them how bad, stupid and incompetent we think they are. We act as if they need to be taught a lesson, and our job is to play teacher. Your new goal is to let these feelings go as soon as you can.

> Interrupt your obsessive thinking by forcing yourself to change the channel on the television of your mind. Force yourself to think about something else.

Do not tell the story again and again of how you were wronged. A slogan that might be helpful is, "Anger is a poison I take to get even with you." In other words, it is like seeking revenge by taking poison and waiting for the person you are angry at to die. Stop taking the poison because it is killing you.

11. Practice losing—not winning.

One of the ideas that can work against us in creating a happy marriage is the idea that marriage is like a football game. The arguments you get into with your spouse (that you say you want to avoid) will require you to relinquish the idea that you should never give up, back down or lose. You may "win" every argument and end up losing your wife.

Many men were raised with the idea that winning *is* the goal. While we may become quite wealthy through striving to win, our relationships with our wives are different from competition at the job or on the playing field of some sport. To gain the respect of our wives, we often need to lose. By "losing" a couple of disagreements, we may "win" a warm, happy weekend.

To gain the respect of our wives, we often need to lose.

> A popular slogan in some of my men's groups has been, "Winning by losing."

12. Practice being wrong—not right.

There is a saying, "You can either be happy or you can be right, but you can't be both." One of my clients was trying to help another man in the group by changing the slogan to, "You can either be right or you can be married, but you can't be both." The man who said that is still happily married five years later. The man who argued against it is divorced and having trouble in his next marriage.

> It is important that we ragers stop standing up for what we think is "the truth" and the "right way."

A man who is very active in his church said to me once, "When we get back together, my wife is going to have to swear that divorce is not an option. Divorce is against the will of God."

I suggested to him that he refocus his values and begin to put more emphasis on humility and kindness and less energy on telling his wife what "the will of God is." I asked him to find some value in her position by telling her the good that came out of her filing for divorce three months earlier. The group helped him see that he could thank his wife for filing for divorce because it really got his attention and helped him to see how important she and the kids were to him. He could say, "Thank you for filing, honey. I know it took a lot of courage for you to do that and get a court order to get me out of the house. It really got my attention!"

He said he was willing to do that but wondered if he could ask her to drop the assault charge. The group groaned in unison. We suggested that if he wanted to be back in the house by Christmas, then he'd better say, "Whatever you want to do is fine with me. You do what is best for you and makes you feel the most comfortable. I can see how having me on probation for a year could reassure you that I will not go back to my old behavior."

13. Practice humility—not self-righteousness.

The most difficult type of anger to let go of is *self-righteous anger.*

"Don't I have the right to make her see the truth when she is absolutely and totally wrong (and I am absolutely and totally right), or when she is hurting herself?"

Or it may take a more subtle form:

"I ain't no saint. I know I have a long way to go before I can entertain the idea of expressing my anger as a positive, loving act as saints and holy men have done. However, my anger proves my love. Come on, now, you know I love you. I *get* so angry precisely because I love you so much."

Consider these points, outlined by Bo Lozoff:[21]

- I no longer believe in the philosophy that my mother was taught as a child, my father was taught as a child, and I was taught as a child; I no longer believe that anger proves love.

- I no longer believe that anger makes me a more interesting person.

- I believe that my ranting and raving is a form of violence.

- I believe that anger never helps.

- I pray every morning, "Please, dear God, allow me to give up anger as my contribution toward a more peaceful world." After my morning prayer, I remind myself that I no longer believe I need my anger. I no longer believe that anger protects me.

- I believe that anger is a false sense of security. But don't I need some healthy anger? While I pray with one hand to let go of anger, with the other I hold on to it for "emergencies." Such security is false and deceptive.

- It's amazing how reluctant (or even terrified) I am to accept a peaceful life—while spending almost all of my time seeking for it to be so.

14. Practice being compassionate—not angry at injustice toward others.

> "If we use anger at injustice as the source for our energy, we may do something harmful, something that we will later regret...Compassion is the only source of energy that is safe. With compassion, your energy is born from insight; it is not blind energy."
> —Thich Nhat Hanh, Vietnamese Buddhist Zen Master, nominated by Martin Luther King for the Nobel Peace Prize in 1968

Angry men run off the genetic programming of our jungle ancestors. However, there are seldom real lions and tigers we need to fight. If we saved our rage and aggression for lions and tigers, then we would be alright. Our problem is that we react to our wives and children disagreeing with us as if they were a lion or a tiger.

Some of us are afraid that if we don't stay in practice with our rage, then there will come a time when we will really need it and it will be unavailable. If someone kicks in your front door, then you may really need it. However, breaking into a rage at that point may also not be the appropriate response and may put you and your family in greater danger. You may want to think back to when you really needed your rage and it really helped you. I can think of hundreds of times when it caused me and others harm, but I cannot think of one time in my life when it was helpful.

> I tell my angry clients that they don't have to worry;
> their anger is not going to disappear altogether.
> Completely losing their anger will not be the problem.

We have been too ready for conflict and have actually looked forward to it. We need to learn how to be more alert to possibilities for reconciliation—not just an end to conflict but for the purpose of a greater harmony. The following story illustrates the need to grow in that direction:

The train clanked and rattled through the suburbs of Tokyo on a drowsy spring afternoon. Our car was comparatively empty—a few housewives with their kids in tow, some old folks going shopping. I gazed absently at the drab houses and dusty hedgerows.

At one station the doors opened, and suddenly the afternoon quiet was shattered by a man bellowing violent, incomprehensible curses. The man staggered into our car. He wore laborer's clothing, and he was big, drunk, and dirty. Screaming, he swung at a woman holding a baby. The blow sent her spinning into the laps of an elderly couple. It was a miracle that the baby was unharmed.

Terrified, the couple jumped up and scrambled toward the other end of the car. The laborer aimed a kick at the retreating back of the old woman but missed as she scuttled to safety. This so enraged the drunk that he grabbed the metal pole in the center of the car and tried to wrench it out of its stanchion. I could see that one of his hands was cut and bleeding. The train lurched ahead, the passengers frozen with fear. I stood up.

I was young then, some 20 years ago, and in pretty good shape. I'd been putting in a solid eight hours of Aikido training nearly every day for the prior three years. I liked to throw and grapple. I thought I was tough. The trouble was, my martial skill was untested in actual combat. As students of Aikido, we were not allowed to fight.

"Aikido," my teacher had said again and again, "is the art of reconciliation. Whoever has the mind to fight has broken his connection with the universe. If you try to dominate people, you are already defeated. We study how to resolve conflict, not how to start it."

I listened to his words. I tried hard. I even went so far as to cross the street to avoid the chimpira, the pinball punks who lounged around the train stations. My forbearance exalted me. I felt both tough and holy. In my heart, however, I wanted an absolutely legitimate opportunity whereby I might save the innocent by destroying the guilty.

"This is it," I said to myself as I got to my feet. "People are in danger. If I don't do something fast, somebody will probably get hurt."

Seeing me stand up, the drunk recognized a chance to focus his rage. "Aha," he roared. "A foreigner. You need a lesson in Japanese manners."

I held on lightly to the commuter strap overhead and gave him a slow look of disgust and dismissal. I planned to take this turkey apart, but he had to make the first move. I wanted him mad, so I pursed my lips and blew him an insolent kiss.

"All right," he hollered. "You're gonna get a lesson." He gathered himself for a rush at me.

A fraction of a second before he could move, someone shouted, "Hey." It was earsplitting. I remember the strangely joyous, lilting quality of it—as though you and a friend had been searching diligently for something, and he had suddenly stumbled upon it. "Hey."

I wheeled to my left; the drunk spun to his right. We both stared down at a little, old Japanese man. He must have been well into his seventies, this tiny gentleman, sitting there immaculate in his kimono. He took no notice of me, but beamed delightedly at the laborer, as though he had a most important, most welcome secret to share.

"C'mere," the old man said in an easy vernacular, beckoning to the drunk. "C'mere and talk with me." He waved his hand lightly.

The big man followed, as if on a string. He planted his feet belligerently in front of the old gentleman, and roared above the clacking wheels, "Why the hell should I talk to you?" The drunk now had his back to me. If his elbow moved so much as a millimeter, I'd drop him in his socks.

The old man continued to beam at the laborer. "What'cha been drinkin'?" he asked, his eyes sparkling with interest.

"I been drinkin' sake," the laborer bellowed back, "and it's none of your business." Flecks of spittle spattered the old man.

"Oh, that's wonderful," the old man said, "absolutely wonderful. You see, I love sake too. Every night, me and my wife (she's seventy-six, you know), we warm up a little bottle of sake and take it out into the garden, and we sit on an old wooden bench. We watch the sun go down, and we look to see how our persimmon tree is doing. My great-grandfather planted that tree, and we worry about whether it will recover from those ice storms we had last winter. Our tree has done better than I expected, though, especially when you consider the poor quality of the soil. It is gratifying to watch when we take our sake and go out to enjoy the evening— even when it rains." He looked up at the laborer, eyes twinkling.

As he struggled to follow the old man's conversation, the drunk's face began to soften. His fists slowly unclenched. "Yeah," he said. "I love persimmons, too..." His voice trailed off.

"Yes," said the old man, smiling, "and I'm sure you have a wonderful wife."

"No," replied the laborer. "My wife died." Very gently, swaying with the motion of the train, the big man began to sob. "I don't got no wife, I don't got no home, I don't got no job. I'm so ashamed of myself." Tears rolled down his cheeks; a spasm of despair rippled through his body.

Now it was my turn. Standing there in my well-scrubbed youthful innocence, my make-this-world-safe-for-democracy righteousness, I suddenly felt dirtier than he was.

Then the train arrived at my stop. As the doors opened, I heard the old man cluck sympathetically. "My, my," he said, "that is a difficult predicament, indeed. Sit down here and tell me about it."

I turned my head for one last look. The laborer was sprawled on the seat, his head in the old man's lap. The old man was softly stroking the filthy, matted hair.

As the train pulled away, I sat down on a bench. What I had wanted to do with muscle had been accomplished with kind words. I had just seen Aikido tried in combat, and the essence of it was love. I would have to practice the art with an entirely different spirit. It would be a long time before I could speak about the resolution of conflict.[22]

15. Practice being persistent in dealing with your anger— not, "How much do you want me to take?"

"Whosoever unceasingly strives upward...him can we save."
— Goethe

"Whether you think you can or think you can't, you're right."
—Anonymous

The work toward changing the principles on which you live your life requires persistence and diligence. These new principles will bring you rewards, but only with persistence.

Not all the men who come to see me are able to save their marriages. For some women it is too late. They are determined to get divorced, no matter what changes their husbands make. Most of the men in this category stay in the group and work on their anger problem. They say they know they have to change this pattern in their life whether the marriage works or not.

In one group, the following dialogue occurred:

Therapist: "What do you want to share with the group tonight?"

Bert: "I am beginning to lose interest in saving this marriage."

Therapist: "You are kidding! After all you have been through? Why is that?"

Bert: "I have done a lot of changing, but her warmth and spontaneity have just not come back in six months. I am tired of being rejected."

Therapist: "What do you plan to do?"

Bert: "I am not sure, but I'm thinking I may take the principles and techniques that I've learned in here and apply them to a rich woman."

Group: (Laughter)

Therapist: "Are you serious?"

Bert: "Well, at least I could find someone who likes me and thinks I am cute or funny. We don't have any children, so I think I'm ready to move on down the road unless she is ready to begin to forgive me."

Therapist: "It sounds like it's time for the three of us to get together and talk about where she is with this marriage."

When we met, they decided that they wanted to be friends but that the marriage was over. Neither of them wanted to try to work it out anymore. Too many therapists for too long, they said. The good news is that Bert is still attending group and practicing his techniques and principles for his next relationship. He says he is in better shape than he has ever been in his life to have a relationship that really works. I agree.

The following excerpts are from correspondence between R., a 27-year-old man and Bo, a spiritual teacher who corresponds with convicts. R. is serving life without parole plus 20 years for three murders and two robberies committed when he was 16. It is enlightening in terms of persistence:

Dear Bo,

Greetings brother. I just want to say thank you; for being a friend, for caring, for sharing your wisdom and insight, for your dedication to those of us society thinks are not worth it.

Thank you for providing me with the tools to aid me in changing my attitude. I'm changing in many subtle ways.

My attitude is improving, the lines in my face are fading. I don't feel so angry all the time, and many other things are changing as well.

Am I still struggling? Of course I am. But I have a goal now that I am struggling for, whereas I was just going blindly before. I am staying focused and not letting the everyday little annoyances get to me. Even the guards say they can see a major change in my attitude.

I realize I have a long journey ahead of me, and I am just beginning. But I have no doubt that I will make it through to the end. I have never done anything half-assed and I'm not going to start now. I have put 100% effort into screwing up the last 27 years of my life; I intend to put 110% into making sure I don't make the same mistakes again.

Is it easy? Hell no. We are creatures of habit and in my opinion, a habit is the hardest thing in the world to break. So I must overcome each habit one by one, and replace the old habit with a new, good habit. It is hard, but with each old one I replace, it becomes a little easier.

As I told you in the past, my most serious problems are an intense anger and hatred—for this place, for the system, for society, and for me. Well, I still hate the system, it is a degenerative, destructive system. I no longer have so much hatred for society, and I no longer hate myself so much.

The anger is another story. I still have a lot of anger in me, but I'm learning to control it, and not let it control me. I am using it as my energy, my motivation, instead of letting it destroy me. I think anger and love are the two most powerful emotions. Both have motivated people to do great things, to make major changes, to become stronger, better, and both have caused many people to do stupid things.

Love & Peace brother,
R.

Dear R.,

I think you're doing great, R. You know you're going to be in prison for a while and you know your own strengths and weaknesses pretty well. Your motivation to do good time instead of bad time is strong. You have a good mind and good heart. You have spiritual friends and teachers. And the most important thing is, you know you have a long way to go.

You want and need to love people and to love life, and you already sort of do. It'll be nice when you admit it to yourself. That's the journey you are on, just like me.

Your Loving brother,
Bo[23]

16. Practice understanding—not explaining.

I counseled with a man a number of years ago who had slapped his nine-year-old boy. A school counselor called Children's Protective Services, which resulted in his arrest. His wife filed for divorce the next day.

Bob seemed to have an intuitive sense that explaining his actions was like digging himself deeper into a hole. When he began seeing the kids after the separation, he concentrated on having fun with his son, Bobby, and his seven-year-old daughter, Karen. The kids reported to their mother that, "Daddy is not mean like he used to be. We are having fun together."

Bob reported that his wife invited him in to talk with her. She said that she felt like she had to file for divorce. He agreed that what she had done made sense to him. He wondered how she had put up with his constant yelling and criticism for all those years.

It wasn't until I pressed him in our second meeting that Bob told me that his son had spit in his face and he had reacted automatically by slapping him. His son, Bobby, had become violent with his wife and he had intervened and taken him into the bedroom to talk to him about settling down.

I said that it would have been difficult for most people to restrain themselves in that situation. I was impressed that he was not indignant about being arrested. He replied, "I don't want to spend another ounce of energy and time justifying my angry and violent behavior." I replied that he was an inspiration to me.

17. Practice feeling awkward—not feeling natural.

> Long-time members of my men's groups laugh when a new member asks, "When do I get to start being myself?"
>
> The answer is, "Never. That's how you got here—by being yourself."

My groups are not traditional psychotherapy. The purpose is for angry men to get support in trying on new behaviors. It takes a while for these behaviors to start to feel natural. Feeling awkward is a sign that you are doing something new. A willingness to experience awkwardness is a sign of a man's love for his wife and family.

There is one time I take up for men in my marital therapy sessions. When the wife says, "He is saying nice things and they sound sincere, but how do I know he really means them?" Although it is progress for a 50-year-old man to be saying things he has never said in his life, and that for sure he never heard his father say to his mother, it is good to be suspicious. I call this loving mistrust. I suggest that his wife reward him with a smile and a, "Thank you." It doesn't really matter if he doesn't mean it. It may take more love and courage to say nice things when he does not mean it.

18. Practice balancing your life—not careerism.

[Eliminate] your TV,
Throw away your paper.
Move to the country,
Build you a home.
Plant a little garden,
Eat a lot of peaches.
Try to find God,
On your own.   *—John Prine*

One of the questions I ask married couples in therapy is how many hours a week they work. One father with two children under five said he worked 80 hours a week. His wife worked 60. They wanted to know if I could help them with their anger and rage at each other.

I told them that I doubted I could unless they were willing to cut back on the hours they worked. They were trial lawyers on the rise in their professions. I saw a courtroom scene a few weeks later on the 10 o'clock news. I recognized the defense attorney as the man who had been in my office. I felt sadness at the price he had paid to become a $500-an-hour criminal defense lawyer.

Ragers cannot work 80 hours a week and still expect to stay married. Two things that are necessary ingredients to recover from rageaholism are sleep and relaxation.

Ask yourself this: Am I more contented every day? Do I have a quiet joy? Am I becoming a bigger, wider, deeper human being of peace and joy on a daily basis? Or am I feeling like it's right around the corner, and I have just to knock myself out for a few more days, weeks, months, years, and then some mystical day I'm going to be open to my peace and joy? Peace starts now or it never starts.

> Contentedness is absolutely one of the most important qualities a human can possess. This quality is not opposed to a dynamic, active lifestyle.

A joyful, contented life is our true nature. Life can be rich and rewarding, but we have to give up our constant demand for more, bigger, newer, better. That demand, observes Lozoff, is literally killing us.[24]

19. Practice staying on the path—not cursing your luck.

Clients often ask me how long it took me to get over my anger. My reply is that I have good news and bad news. First the good news. I have gotten over enough of my anger to be happily married and lead a good life. This is more than I ever thought possible. I am grateful for that.

The bad news is that I will probably be working on this problem for the rest of my life. I am "wired hot." I have always gotten excited easily. I have always been impulsive. I was a righteous, religious kid who thought he was better than everyone else. Working on these problems is my spiritual path. It may not be everyone's, but it has been mine now for about 15 years. I sometimes say, "I have turned a character defect into a full-time career. Now I have turned it into a book."

20. Practice daily spiritual meditation—not sleeping late.

> *"Therefore, I will put this way of life into actual practice. For what can be achieved by merely talking about it? Will a sick man be benefited merely by reading the medical text?"*
>
> —Shantideva

Spending a few minutes every morning in some kind of regular spiritual practice can be an important part of changing our behavior. I know how unbelievably hard it is to change our lives in major ways. I know how easy it is to be cynical about trying yet one more round of ideas or practices or vows or New Year's resolutions. We've failed so many times.

> *"But on our way toward becoming free of all habitual behavior, it is often necessary first to replace bad habits with good ones. The habit of spiritual practice—especially at the very beginning of each day— can remind us of who we are and what we wish our lives to be about."*
>
> —Bo Lozoff[25]

Pursuing spiritual principles requires practice. We need some way to remind ourselves daily so that we do not fall back into old familiar habits of thinking, feeling and talking. We need to do something different to keep ourselves on track. Something more than you are doing now. What you have been doing has not worked. Any conception of God, higher power or universal spirit is not relevant to what we are talking about here. We are interested in a practice that reminds us of where we want to go on our journey. There needs to be some kind of daily commitment to remind ourselves to review these principles so we can begin to develop awareness.

The Vietnamese Zen master, Thich Nhat Hanh, suggests that you not practice expressing anger. He suggests instead that you visualize yourself as a garden. The anger is imagined as a weed that you do not want to water. What you do want to water are feelings of compassion and love. He suggests that you may need to look for some kind of a daily practice that will water these plants of compassion and love and not water the weeds of anger, hatred, bitterness, revenge, self-pity, self-hate and time urgency. All are weeds in our interior garden.

Thich Nhat Hanh suggests a daily practice of tuning into your breathing for a few minutes a day. You can breathe in thinking the phrase: "Breathing in, I know that I am angry." Then breathe out with the phrase, "Breathing out, I send the world peace." Do that for 20 seconds or 20 minutes with your eyes closed. When your anger disappears, then you can change your phrase to, "Breathing in, I am aware that I am breathing in." On the out breath say silently to yourself, "Breathing out, I am aware that I am breathing out."

If you want to use prayer as a spiritual practice, it may help to make your prayer as specific as possible. After working on my anger in every therapy imaginable for over 10 years, I was only 50 percent better. One day on the first vacation after our marriage, I lost my temper at my wife over her not answering me when I asked, "Aren't those pretty trees?" I screamed and yelled and pounded the dashboard in our little Mazda RX-7, cursing and calling her names. She had already been irritated at me for drinking all the water before she got back from her jog on a hot August day in Texas. I knew that I was in big trouble. I was afraid I was going to end up getting divorced again. The next day she said that if that ever happened again, she would leave. I replied, "I know."

I knew that I could not take a chance of even starting to express any anger for the next 90 days. The next morning I started saying a simple prayer out loud on my knees, "God, help me today not to speak one single word of profanity at any time for any reason, no matter what, *no matter what.*" All my psychological therapies had failed me. I could not do this through good intentions, apologies and solemn oaths. At night I prayed, "God, I thank you for your support today in not speaking one single word of profanity." If I had slipped during the day, no matter how slight or justified, I acknowledged it at this point and recommitted to absolutely no profanity. It worked. Within 10 days, I had stopped a 30-year habit. I was on my way to a happy marriage. I have had only a few slips in the last 10 years.

My suggestion is that you pray for something specific if you are going to pray every morning for changes in your angry behavior. At night you can thank God for his support. Then acknowledge your slips and commit again to no profanity.

The New Testament admonishes us to, "let all bitterness, wrath, anger, clamor and evil speaking be put away from you with all malice and be kind to another. Tender hearted, forgiving one another even as God for Christ's sake has forgiven you."[26] This is a scripture that you could sit quietly and repeat for 10 minutes every day.

Another option is to repeat any prayer meditatively each day. Actually you may take any prayer—one word, phrase or sentence at a time—and repeat it in the morning meditatively, then over and over as you drive to work.

The man who wrote the following prayer is considered a saint, but you need not let that put you off. He had gone through the wringer emotionally and this is a prayer he created when he had come out the other side. A good way to start is to take the first phrase of this prayer and repeat it softly out loud to yourself, if you are alone. If not, then think it silently:

"Lord make me a channel of thy peace." You can close your eyes and visualize yourself as a channel of peace wherever you go today (home, office, freeway, subway or store). You may want to imagine that a white light radiates from your chest and brings peace to everyone near you. You may want to meditate on this one phrase for the whole day.

"That where there is hatred, I may bring love." This is phrase two of what is known as the Saint Francis prayer. You can imagine scenes where you may be facing hatred today. See yourself bringing love to these situations.

"That where there is wrong, I may bring the spirit of forgiveness." You can think of times when you may have been wronged. See if at this moment you can bring the spirit of forgiveness to the scene where you have been wronged.

"That where there is discord, I may bring harmony." See yourself as being quiet and patient, talking softly in a situation where one or two others are yelling and cursing.

"That where there is error, I may bring truth." Now do not use this to hurt others or become righteous. Where you have made an error, you need to tell the truth about it. Don't focus on what you imagine to be the other person's error. You will make plenty of errors today like all the rest of us. And this is an opportunity to tell the truth about them. You may want to imagine a situation where you made an error in the last few days that you haven't acknowl-

edged to someone else. You may want to consider acknowledging that and telling the truth about it today.

"That where there is doubt, I may bring faith." When you doubt you can be a kind, gentle person, start with whatever faith you can. Faith is action fueled by doubt.

"That where there is despair, I may bring hope." When you despair that your rage will continue to ruin your life and relationships, bring hope that you can do as others have done before and develop a kinder and gentler way.

"That where there are shadows, I may bring light." Inside you, where there are shadows of depression and vengeance, bring light. Imagine light going into those parts of you where there are shadows of resentments that you consider justified.

"That where there is sadness, I may bring joy." Start by bringing yourself joy. One of the best ways is gratitude. For the next few breaths that you exhale, you may want to express gratitude for some current blessings in your life.

"Lord, grant that I may seek rather to comfort than to be comforted." This would be a time to imagine yourself sympathizing and saying to your wife, "That must be difficult."

"To understand, than to be understood." You could imagine yourself giving up trying to be understood and getting sympathy for your position and instead repeating back to your wife what you hear her saying so that she can hear that you understand.

"To love than to be loved." You might want to focus on what kind of behavior on your part makes your wife feel loved rather than arguing for her to do what makes you feel loved.

"For it is by self-forgetting that one finds." The path to happiness and peace for us angry men is getting the attention off what we want or feel we deserve.

"It is by forgiving that one is forgiven." Most of us ragers have behaved in ways for which we very much want to be forgiven. The way to attain this forgiveness is to start practicing forgiveness.

"It is by dying that one awakens to eternal life." Our pride, accomplishments, and bank accounts are not part of what is eternal.

"Amen."

—The St. Francis Prayer[27]

In Summary...

Believing in these principles is important because in order to give abstinence meaning, I had to see a higher meaning for my actions. Often we angry men lose the bigger picture and the bigger goal and impulsively give in to our anger. These beliefs allow us to center and ground ourselves in something bigger than our own selfish wants.

PRACTICE THESE PRINCIPLES

1. Practice self-restraint—don't always express yourself.
2. Practice kindness—not revenge.
3. Practice being gracious—not critical.
4. Practice self-examination—not blame.
5. Practice empathy—not selfishness.
6. Practice surrendering—not dominating.
7. Practice service to others—not self-interest.
8. Practice disciplining yourself—not "I have to have my way."
9. Practice being patient—not impulsive.
10. Practice forgiveness—not punishment.
11. Practice losing—not winning.
12. Practice being wrong—not right.
13. Practice humility—not self-righteousness.
14. Practice being compassionate—not angry at injustice toward others.
15. Practice being persistent in dealing with your anger—not "How much do you want me to take?"
16. Practice understanding—not explaining.
17. Practice feeling awkward—not feeling natural.
18. Practice balancing your life—not careerism.
19. Practice staying on the path—not cursing your luck.
20. Practice daily spiritual meditation—not sleeping late.

CHAPTER 3

C = COMMUNICATE

COMMUNICATE WITH THESE NEW PHRASES

Consider the following "scripts" for talking with your partner, some for *deep doghouse communication* and some for *shallow doghouse communication.*

Deep Doghouse Communication

> *"Whatever we learn to do we learn by actually doing it. Builders by building and harp players by playing the harp. In the same way by doing just acts we learn to be just. By doing self-controlled acts we come to be self-controlled. And by doing brave acts, we become brave."*
>
> —Aristotle

Many times when an angry or rageful man comes into the office to see me for the first visit, he is in a deep crisis. Such was the case with Jerry. He was in the "deep doghouse." He was separated from his wife and she had filed for divorce. A man is in the *deep doghouse* when his wife is very angry and most of the communication is her expressing anger, displeasure and criticism of him.

Although Jerry was deep in the doghouse, he was what I call an eager customer. He was not interested in spending the session explaining to me how he was right and she was wrong. Neither was he particularly interested in exploring his psychological make-up or that of his wife.

Jerry was an engineer with 20 years at a big oil company. Often, therapists complain of engineers because they are slow to get in touch with their feelings. However, engineers are my favorite clients because they put the pressure on me to provide something that works and works quickly. He wanted something to prove to his wife that he was making a dramatic change.

We discussed the importance of abstaining from the 15 behaviors that trigger rageaholics. Jerry said that he would work to control his behavior. He said that he would not be in this predicament if he had been abstaining from these behaviors all along, especially profanity.

The next week he said that things were no worse with his wife and he had not lost his temper. I complimented Jerry on his good work. He had done a great job of not exploding, even when his wife was cursing him and calling him names. Jerry went to great lengths to stop his profanity, name-calling, mocking and threatening, and he even kept a quiet voice.

When I asked him what he wanted to get out of the next session, he said, "I want to learn how to stop arguing with her, if that is possible." He said that they kept having very long arguments that went on for hours on the phone. I told Jerry that there were three words that would stop any argument: "You are right."

"You are right."

These words will stop an argument because in order to have an argument, there has to be a disagreement. Without a disagreement, it is impossible to have an argument. Now these words go against some of our training as men. What we men have learned is how to hang on to being right. I was told that I should never give up when I was right. I was taught to stick to what I believed. And this idea of sticking with what you believe, never stopping, hanging on to being right, may be useful in many areas of your life, but I think you have probably found that it is not useful in your marriage.

Most of you may be thinking, "But what if she isn't right? Am I supposed to lie?" I suggest that you:

1. Say the phrase, "You are right."

2. Find *some truth* in what she is saying and agree with it.

3. Get your "but" out of the way. Don't say: "You are right, but..."

You can state your opinion when you get out of the doghouse.

The truth of the matter is, no matter what anyone says, you can always find some smidgen of truth in it. You can acknowledge she is right in some way.

When I worked at the VA hospital's inpatient unit for substance abusers, new patients would often repeatedly say in group therapy, "Not me; that is not true. That is not true about me." The staff used this as a sign that they were not making progress. Even though some had lived on the streets as junkies for several years, they claimed to have no problems and were reluctant to examine themselves.

Weekend passes were approved based on the patient's progress in the therapy group during the week. When I would refuse a weekend pass to a "not me" patient, he would often say he didn't understand what he was supposed to do.

I would say, "Well, I will play you a game of psychological ping-pong for a pass." Now how would psychological ping-pong go? The patient would be first and he would say something negative about me: "Newton you are a selfish, self-centered, egotistical guy."

The rule was that I had to begin my answer with three words: "You are right," then repeat what he said and give an example of how he was right. I would say, "You are right, John. I am a selfish, self-centered, egotistical guy. Last weekend I insisted that my wife and I go to the movie that I wanted to see."

The group would judge whether I passed. Then it would be my turn. I would say, "John, you are a hard-headed junkie who is going to die shooting dope under a bridge." And he would say (even though he didn't live under a bridge and lived in a nice home), "Newton, you are right. I am a hard-headed junkie. I will die shooting dope living under a bridge if I don't change my ways."

The idea is for each person to begin to find truth in what the other person says. The person who loses is the person who is unable to repeat what the other person says and give an example.

As you can imagine, as the intensity of the game increases, some pretty rough things are said about the other person. The point is that it breaks the habit, the mindset with which we men were trained—to fight for our idea of the truth and argue on and on. We need to learn a more flexible way to deal with criticism.

My friend Paul laughed at me one day in graduate school because I kept getting into a conflict with a professor and losing—week after week. He said that it was like watching an old Western movie. I would charge at her and she would just step aside. I would go flying out the window and splatter on the sidewalk below. He said that I approached the conflict more like John Wayne and she approached it like a Judo master. He found it fun to watch her use my force and not resist.

Sometimes we get confused at this point, thinking that if we say to our wives, "You are right," we have to go along with whatever they want us to do. "You are right" does not mean you agree to change anything. I say this over and over again—and it is hard for most ragers to comprehend. Someone telling me that I am selfish, self-centered and egotistical is not a request for a behavioral change. These are universal, human frailties. I make no commitment to change any behavior when I agree with her that I am selfish, self-centered and egotistical. It is not the time to argue when you are deep in the doghouse and your wife is ranting and raving at you.

A lot of men feel ashamed or shamed by these kinds of words. And a lot of us, as John Bradshaw says, have our shame tanks full, so we find it hard to take on any more shame. So when someone calls us selfish, self-centered and egotistical, we feel we must turn our shame into anger instantly because the experience of shame is too excruciating for us. Some variations of "You are right" include "You are right, sweetheart," "You are absolutely right, sweetheart," or "I agree; you are right."

One of my clients, Ralph, is good at this skill. During a session, his wife Laura said, "You don't even care about your family or your kids." He replied, "You are right. There are lots more things I could do for you and the kids. I would love to spend all day Saturday with just the four of us." Ralph kept saying the right things. "I have not spent a lot of time with you and the kids in the past and there have been many times where I have chosen my own selfish, self-centered interests over yours and the kids."

When deep in the doghouse, you should not explain your behavior, nor defend your behavior and certainly not counterattack. Deep doghouse communication is about receiving the message and validating her point of view. It is about receiving, not sending. Arguments get started when you try to send back when she is still sending. If you say, "Well, you haven't always been around here either. How about the two weeks you went to visit your mother?" That is gasoline on the fire.

I counseled a man who told me he was willing to do anything to save his marriage. After seeing him a few times, I suggested that he bring his wife in because she had agreed to give him another chance to show that he was able to change. The way I set up the session was that she was to say two or three sentences at a time to him about anything that she wanted to. As it happened, she brought a long list. He was to begin his sentences with, "You are right, sweetheart" and give an example of how she was right. He did that without exception for 45 minutes. She was impressed. This showed significant change.

The *CBSSW* Phrases

There is an acronym I suggest for answers to "why" questions. The acronym is *CBSSW*. That acronym was thought up by a men's group to answer their wives' question: "Why did you do that again?"

There are two separate rounds for using this acronym. In round one, the answers to "why" questions are C ("I was *crazy*"), B ("I was *bad*"), S ("I was *stupid*"), S ("I was *sick*") and W ("I was *wrong*"). If the "why" questions continue, you can go back to the beginning and expand your answers (round two). Responses for round two include:

"I am crazy."

"I was completely crazy. You are absolutely right; it was a very bad thing I did."

"I couldn't agree with you more. I am sick; something is wrong with me."

"I was stupid to have done that."

"I was wrong; you are right."

"I don't know what is wrong with me."

Again, the *CBSSW* mantra is:

"I am crazy."

"I am bad."

"I am stupid."

"I am sick."

"I am wrong."

You may need to practice saying the words that you have never said in your life—and that you never heard your father say—namely, "I am wrong." I often remind myself that when I am *right*, I am dangerous. I am better off being wrong.

One thing that happens when your spouse is angry with you because you have broken an agreement is that she will ask you "why" questions. "Why did you do this?" "Why did you do that?" This is a temptation for you to send an explanation of your behavior, but if you send an explanation, you are in trouble. "Why" questions are really not about inviting an explanation.

Let me give you an example. Let's say when I was four years old, I spilled my milk at the dinner table. My father says, "Newton, why did you do that?"

Now if I had given an explanation like, "I really don't have the small muscle coordination in my right hand that most four year olds have since I'm a little bit developmentally delayed on my hand coordination," he would not have been happy. In fact, he would have been furious. Actually, a "why" question is often an attempt to shame the person and to tell him he is bad or wrong. If you think of this as Judo instead of John Wayne, you will work yourself out of the doghouse.

Matthew's wife, Betty, angrily asked him: "Why did you lose your temper at the kids again? Why did you lose your temper again after you swore and promised me that you would never do it again? Why did you do that?"

The two ways that Matthew avoided having an argument were: 1) He did not start to explain that the kids would not listen. 2) He did not answer Betty's "why" question with a "why" question like "Betty, why can't you ever stop criticizing me?" Instead, Matthew practiced the first two phrases in deep doghouse communication:

Matthew: "You are right, honey. I shouldn't have lost my temper."

Betty: "Well, then why did you?"

Matthew: "I am *crazy* to keep blowing up when I know you are about to divorce me."

Betty: "You are crazy to scream the things you do at your kids and then say you love them. It's just not right."

Matthew: "It was a *bad* thing I did. I agree. I am *bad* to do those kinds of things over and over."

Betty: "You don't make any sense. You say the right things when we go to therapy, then you keep screwing up."

Matthew: "I know I am *stupid* to keep making the same mistake."

Betty: "I think you are just plain nuts. You must be mentally ill to think I am going to continue to raise my kids around some maniac like you."

Matthew: "I agree. I am *sick*. That is the only explanation I can think of."

Betty: "Something is wrong with you, that's for sure. You had better get it fixed."

Matthew: "I am *wrong* to have let it happen again. I don't know what is the matter with me."

Some people react to this technique with horror saying that it is teaching insincerity and lying, that I am making men worse psychopaths than they already are. Some therapists particularly take issue with this approach because they feel it subverts honest communication.

My first response is that some angry and violent men don't need to be taught open expression of anger. Some need to be locked up instead. My idea is that it is more important that some of us learn to take a one-down position in our marriage than it is to tell the truth about every angry feeling. Telling the truth about our angry feelings and expressing them were part of the therapy invented for depressed women. There is nothing sacred about that therapy. Angry men need to learn to contain their feelings and to practice agreeing with and finding truth in what their wives say.

My second response is, "Fake it 'till you make it." If some people want to call it lying about your feelings, then I say to my clients, "Lie. It would be better than what you are doing now."

Another criticism I frequently receive contends I am shaming men by suggesting they say those horrible things about themselves. The reason for men's anger, these therapists believe, is that the men have underlying shame and my techniques make it worse.

My response to friends and colleagues in the men's movement is "You are right. A lot of men are full of guilt and shame. It is important that we get over it if we are going to have a happy life. I do not want to do anything to make men feel worse about themselves." My clients are not coming in to work on their inner child. They are coming to stay married and learn to be happily married. I have found that admitting to common human frailties such as crazy, bad, stupid, sick and wrong has been a big relief for me. We no longer have to pretend that there is *nothing* wrong with us or defend ourselves.

I spent years trying to prove I wasn't a crazy person. I was afraid it would be bad for my psychotherapy practice for people to "find out." Now when clients tell me, "Newton, I think you are crazy," I say that is not new information; I have known that for years. I gave up on trying to be sane a number of years ago. What I have found is a way to be happy in life and be happily married and I would be glad to teach them what I know. The goal of my therapy is not sanity, but happiness.

Some clients are surprised to discover that I have had a really bad anger problem, sometimes worse than theirs. They will sometimes say, "My God, I believe you have been sicker than I ever was." Of course, I say, "You are right. My anger problem is much worse than yours. You have a light case compared to mine. Boy, are you lucky."

This teaching does not mean always taking a one-down position, nor does it mean always doing what your wife wants you to do. It means being able to take a one-down position verbally more consistently. Also it means cheerfully doing what your wife wants you to do some of the time.

Anger-Busting Therapy is based on the idea that you act your way to a better way of feeling and thinking. It is not based on feeling your way to a better way of acting. Therefore, I say, "Fake it 'till you make it."

Some of my clients who are therapy veterans ask me if I am suggesting that they lie about their feelings. My response is, "Lie and suppress yourself. It would be a vast improvement over what you are doing now."

The goal of my therapy is not sanity, but happiness. I don't try to keep people from having crazy thoughts; I help them have satisfying relationships.

Bill O'Hanlon has written an excellent book entitled *Do One Thing Different and Other Uncommonly Sensible Solutions to Life's Persistent Problems.*[28] He suggests a definition of insanity: "Doing the same thing over and over again and expecting different results."

To illustrate this point in a way men can relate to, we periodically sing the *Anger-Busting Theme Song* in therapy sessions and in workshops. Here is the *Anger-Busting Theme Song* (sung to the tune of "If You're Happy and You Know It, Clap Your Hands").

Verse 1
(Before Anger-Busting Therapy)
You say I'm crazy, bad and stupid, sick and wrong?
Not me.
You say I'm crazy, bad and stupid, sick and wrong?
Not me.
You say I'm crazy, bad and stupid. You say I'm crazy, bad and stupid. You say I'm crazy, bad and stupid, sick and wrong?
Not me.

Verse 2
(During Anger-Busting Therapy)
You say I'm crazy, bad and stupid, sick and wrong?

Could be.
You say I'm crazy, bad and stupid, sick and wrong?
Could be.
You say I'm crazy, bad, and stupid. You say I'm crazy, bad and
stupid. You say I'm crazy, bad and stupid, sick and
wrong?
Could be.

Verse 3
(After Anger-Busting Therapy)
Yes, I'm crazy, bad and stupid, sick and wrong.
And happy.
Yes, I'm crazy, bad and stupid, sick and wrong.
And happy.
Yes, I'm crazy, bad and stupid. Yes, I'm crazy, bad and stupid.
Yes, I'm crazy, bad, stupid, sick and wrong.
And happy.

Shallow Doghouse Communication

One communication technique does not fit all situations. The
shallow doghouse techniques are for when your wife is not so angry
at you that she is yelling insults about your personality. Things are
cool in the relationship and she is withdrawn. Maybe you try to give
her a hug and she says, "Don't you dare touch me." That would be a
sign you are still in the doghouse.

Now it may be time to apologize. So the next set of phrases to
learn in your new foreign language is:

"I am really sorry."

"It was all my fault."

"Please forgive me."

"What can I do to make it up to you?"

To continue with Matthew and Betty:

Matthew: "I'm really sorry that I blew up at the kids again. I
           know it's traumatic for them."

Betty: "Yeah. That's what you always say."

Matthew: "It really was all my fault. They didn't deserve it."

Betty: "I know that. I'm glad that you have finally caught
         on."

Matthew: "Please forgive me."

Betty: "I'm tired of forgiving you, especially when you turn around and do it again."

Matthew: "What could I do to make it up to you?"

Now sometimes you get the cold shoulder of silence. Sometimes she will tell you there is nothing you can do...that this time you went too far...there is nothing you could ever do to make it up. I would suggest you ask every two or three days what you could do to make amends. I wouldn't push the question, but it is important to ask it.

Betty: "Are you serious this time? Are you finally willing to do something?"

Matthew: "Yes, I'm serious. What do you want me to do?"

Betty: "I want you to go see my therapist with me next week."

Matthew: "I would be glad to, but you know I don't believe in this counseling stuff."

Betty: "I didn't ask you to believe in it. I just want you to show up. Are you trying to weasel out of it already?"

Matthew: "No, honey. You give me the time, day and directions and I'll be there. If I go to counseling, how much will I be out of the doghouse?"

Betty: "Maybe 50 percent. It will depend on how you do in counseling. You had better stay away from singing the tune of, 'I just can't help it; it just comes over me.' I swear if you ever say that again, I will file for divorce the next day."

If she does make a suggestion, get it translated into something you can do and she can tell you have done it (what therapists call behavioral terms). Typically, "trying harder" is guaranteed to fail because neither one of you knows what that means. "Solemn oaths" come in second as the most useless thing you can agree to do.

Getting out of the doghouse may have nothing to do directly with what you did. A few years ago I had gotten deep in the doghouse. One of the things I put my foot down about was having two inside cats. Gray Kitty was an outside cat and a rather mean one at that. When I got to the line of, "I will do anything to make it up to you, if you will forgive me," my wife said, "Really?"

"Absolutely," I said.

She smiled and walked to the door and opened it. In a cheerful voice she said, "Here, Gray Kitty. You are an inside cat now."

Gray Kitty scampered in and I said, "Oh, no, anything but that."

My wife replied, "Too late now. You said, 'Anything.'"

Gray Kitty is a daily reminder to bite my tongue.

What else could you say to get out of the doghouse besides, "How much longer are you going to keep this up? It was not that big a deal." How about:

"I see you are still upset with me."

"I would really like to hear about it."

Now let's say she responds with, "I don't want to talk about it." This is not a good time to say, "For God's sake, Betty, how long are you going to hang onto this? I didn't commit a crime. All I did was yell at those kids and they had it coming."

What might work better is to say:

"That's okay. When you are ready to talk about it, I want to hear about it."

"I promise just to listen."

So let's say Betty tells you, "I am really upset about you continually losing your temper. I'm really feeling disappointed and hopeless about our marriage. We have gone to counseling and you promised to do better, yet you are not living up to your promises. I can't believe this happened again." Your response might be:

"Let's see if I understood what you said..."

Now repeat back exactly what she said, like you were a mirror—no interpreting and no adding anything about what you thought or meant.

"Did I get what you said?"

If she says, "Yes" when you ask "Did I get what you said?" then you say, "What else?"

"What else?"

Now you listen again to a few sentences and mirror them back until she is through, then you say:

"Thank you for sharing with me. I really appreciate it."

Many men balk at saying these phrases. Some clients say to me: "Newton, I just don't say those kind of things."

My typical response is, "I know you don't. That's why you're here. That's why you spent the night on your buddy's couch last night." With just a small degree of effort you can say these things. You may need to look in the bathroom mirror and put your fingers to your lips to shape them into saying some of these phrases and then practice them. This is the opportunity to practice the spiritual principles of awkwardness and persistence. Of course, these phrases feel weird. They are supposed to. If you were comfortable saying these things, you probably wouldn't need this book anyway. Keep saying them until they feel like *you.*

Change the compliments-to-criticism ratio. The closest you need to get to a criticism is to make a request starting with:

"In the future it would please me if you would..."

Rather than saying, "When are you ever going to remember that I like two percent milk, not this nonfat stuff?" you will say in a sweet tone, "In the future it would please me if you would get me two percent milk."

See if you can go a whole week without saying anything critical to your spouse. Nothing critical. Don't speak the things you think of that could be critical, things that you would prefer to be a different way or things that she could have done better.

Men with anger and rage problems typically believe they were appointed by God to straighten out all the problems of the world. It should be clear now that it is not your job to straighten out your wife by pointing out what she is doing wrong. Instead, I believe that God told me that my real job for the rest of my life is to learn to accept and appreciate my wife just like she is. Learn to love her. Learn to abstain from criticizing her in any way.

"Honey, thank you for..."

It is okay to express the same appreciation every day. You don't have to be original. We men often think if we say something once, that is good enough. We told our wives we loved them 20 years ago when we got married. Why would she want me to tell her again? I told her if I changed my mind, I would let her know...otherwise she should assume that the last communication is still valid.

Expressing appreciation even if you say the same things every day will help sustain your marriage.

"Thank you, honey, for doing such a good job with the kids."

"Thank you, honey, for making a good dinner tonight after you worked all day."

"Thank you, honey, for getting the kids ready on time for school so I can leave on time."

"Thank you for all you do."

"Thank you for cleaning the house this week."

"Thank you for working and bringing home a good paycheck."

"Thank you for taking such good care of yourself."

You can say all those phrases every day. You don't have to be an Einstein to think up something new or original or to say it in a new, original way. Express your appreciation.

On days when you are in a bad mood on the way home, think of three appreciations you are going to say when you walk in the door and kiss your wife hello. Think of three things you are going to tell her you appreciate. And tell her what you appreciate instead of opening the door and saying three things that are wrong or saying nothing at all.

And don't forget this phrase:

"I love you; you are the most beautiful woman in the world."

If your wife says, "You don't really mean that. That's just what that book told you to say," then you are to say, "You are right. The book did give me the idea—and I really mean it. I *do* love you. You *are* the most beautiful woman in the world."

If she says, "Well, the book told you to say that too, you con artist," you respond with, "Sweetheart, just say 'thank you'...you are beginning to hurt my feelings."

In Summary...

Many of us men have lived our lives thinking we should just spit out what we are thinking and that how we say something is not important. That is not the way it is with women. I notice when fishing I will say to my buddy, "Hand me the tackle box." He will do it without saying anything. There is not a problem. If it were my wife, I would say, "Honey, would you mind handing me the tackle box? I would sure appreciate it," then "Thank you." Do what works with your wife. Change the way you talk.

TRY THESE PHRASES FOR:

Deep Doghouse Communication

1. "You are right."
2. "I am crazy."
3. "I am bad."
4. "I am stupid."
5. "I am sick"
6. "I am wrong."

Shallow Doghouse Communication

1. "I am really sorry."
2. "It was all my fault."
3. "Please forgive me."
4. "What can I do to make it up to you?"
5. "I see you are still upset with me."
6. "I would really like to hear about it."
7. "That's okay. When you are ready to talk about it, I want to hear about it."
8. "I promise just to listen."
9. "Let's see if I understood what you said..."
10. "Did I get what you said?"
11. "What else?"
12. "Thank you for sharing with me. I really appreciate it."
13. "In the future it would please me if you would..."
14. "Honey, thank you for..."
15. "I love you; for me you are the most beautiful woman in the world."

SECTION II

DECISION TIME FOR WOMEN:
WHEN TO TRAIN HIM AND WHEN TO DUMP HIM

"God, grant me the serenity to accept the things I cannot change, courage to change the things I can, and wisdom to know the difference."

—Serenity Prayer

118

CHAPTER 4

WHEN TO GET RID OF YOUR MAN AND FORGET ABOUT TRAINING

"...as we look at violence and abuse in the family, our idea of the family changes, from a place of safety to a place of danger, from a context of nurturing to a context of nightmare."[29]

—D. Moltz

We have been raised to think of our home as a place of safety, a refuge from the harsh demands of the outside world. Home is the one place where we are supposed to receive unconditional love, nurturing, acceptance, warmth and support. It is a place where we are meant to feel safe. But for some women, home is the opposite. It is a place of humiliation and verbal and physical abuse. Home is a place of fear. In these homes, women are being ridiculed, humiliated, verbally abused, punched, slapped, pushed, shoved, slammed into walls, burned, knifed, shot, kicked, raped and subjected to all kinds of unimaginable emotional and physical abuse. Home is the nightmare that these women wake up to every day.

There are many stereotypes about which women are more prone to abuse. The most common stereotype involves passive housewives who stay at home and take care of their children. But this is a myth. Battered or abused women don't fall into any one category. They are doctors, lawyers, psychotherapists, blue-collar workers, secretaries, truck drivers, bankers, financial advisors, social workers, athletes, supermodels, entertainers, and businesspeople. Women who suffer abuse can be funny, philosophical, educated, uneducated, short, tall, fat, thin, unattractive, gorgeous, rich or poor. There is no one category for abused women. Women who are abused come from all walks of life.

We don't know exactly how many women are battered or abused since many do not report the incident because of the stigma associated with victimization, the private nature of the event and the belief that there will be no benefit from reporting it. We do know that the majority of battered women don't look to police, doctors or therapists for help. They look to their friends and family. While friends and family genuinely want to help, they often don't know how.

More than four million Americans are victims of domestic violence each year. According to the Federal Bureau of Investigation, about 30 percent of female murder victims (1,500 women) are killed by their husbands, ex-husbands, boyfriends or ex-boyfriends each year. Of the 5,745 women murdered in one year, 6 out of 10 were killed by someone they knew. What we don't know is how many women are permanently maimed or injured as a result of family violence.[30]

> More than twice as many women are killed by their husbands or boyfriends as are murdered by strangers.

Consider this: Of females killed by intimate partners in 1998, 58 percent of women killed were married (2,415). Girlfriends were the next highest percentage (24.5 percent, 1,041), followed by common-law wives (8 percent, 332), ex-wives (4.9 percent, 205), and friends (4.6 percent, 196).

Between 21 and 34 percent of American women are battered by a male partner. Despite the femme fatale portrayed in Hollywood movies like *Fatal Attraction*, women are six times more likely than men to be victimized by a spouse, ex-spouse or boyfriend. According to the National Organization for Women Legal Defense and Education Fund (NOW LDEF), the suffering of battered women does not end with physical abuse alone. Nor does it stay in the home. NOW LDEF reports that between 24 and 30 percent of battered women lose their jobs, due at least in part, to domestic violence. Fifty-six percent of abused women are also harassed by the abuser at work.

Who is at the greatest risk of being battered? The National Crime Victimization Survey[31] found that women between the ages of 19 and 29 experienced the highest rates of battering (21.3 per 1,000 women) as compared to 10.8 per 1,000 for women aged 30-45. Moreover, different types of relationships have different rates of battering. The highest battering rates are in cohabitation (35 out of 100 women), dating (20 out of 100 women), and marriage (15 out of 100 women). The following data from the Domestic Violence Hotline reveals a chilling portrait of domestic violence in the United States:

National Domestic Violence Hotline: Violence Fact Sheet and Statistics[32]

Domestic violence is a leading cause of injury to American women.

More than 3 out of every 100—or 1.8 million—women had been severely assaulted by male partners or cohabitants (i.e., they were punched, kicked, choked, beaten, threatened with a knife or gun, or had a knife or a gun used on them) during the preceding 12 months. Other estimates are that higher proportions of women (between 8.5 and 11.3 women per 100) are abused by husbands or boyfriends in the United States.

A minimum of 16 percent of American couples experienced an assault during the year they were asked about it, and about 40 percent of these involved severely violent acts, such as kicking, biting, punching, choking and attacks with weapons.

Nearly one in eight of the husbands had carried out one or more acts of physical aggression against his wife during the 12 months preceding questioning. About 1 in 3 female victims of violence have been injured as a result of the incident.

Fourteen percent of women reported that a husband or boyfriend had been violent with them.

From a sample of police domestic violence reports in an urban population:[33]

> More than half of the incidents involved partners (spousal and nonspousal), about a fourth involved prior or estranged partners, and the remainder involved family members and relatives.

> Fatal incidents predominantly involved handguns, and nonfatal incidents bodily force.

> Data on prior police contacts suggest that family and intimate assaults occur within a context of repeated violence.

During the last decade, domestic violence has been identified as one of the major causes of emergency room visits by women. Among the findings:

- From 20 to 30 percent of the women who are seen by emergency room physicians exhibit at least one or more symptoms of physical abuse; one-half of all injuries presented by women were the result of a partner's aggression.

- More than one-half of all rapes to women over the age of 30 were partner rapes.

- Ten percent of the victims were pregnant at the time of abuse.

- Ten percent reported that their children had also been abused by the batterer.

- Eighty-six percent of the victims had suffered at least one previous incident of abuse.

- About 40 percent had previously required medical care for abuse.

Emotional abuse can include behaviors like putting down a spouse's physical appearance, ridicule, humiliation, name-calling, treating a female partner like a servant, insensitivity to feelings, jealousy and suspiciousness of friends and blame for a spouse's upset. Karen Stout and Beverly McPhail have looked closely at the emotional impact of abuse in their well-researched volume *Confronting Sexism and Violence Against Women*. For instance, 234 women who had been physically abused were interviewed. Ninety-eight percent of them also reported emotional abuse; 72 percent believed that emotional abuse had affected them more than physical abuse. Ridicule was reported as the most harmful form of emotional abuse.[34]

Emotional abuse is far more common than physical abuse and its consequences are just as devastating.

Emotional abuse takes many forms, as displayed in the "Power and Control Wheel" developed by the Domestic Abuse Intervention Project in Duluth, Minnesota.[35]

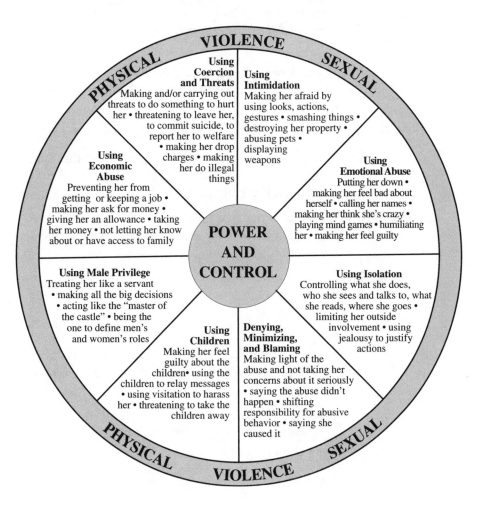

> Angry men frequently use intimidation tactics to frighten their partner and control their behavior. These tactics typically include angry stares, slamming doors, punching or smashing objects, pounding fists on the table, yelling, and infringing on her personal space.

Who batters?

A few years ago I received a call from a woman who said her therapist had suggested that she call me. The conversation went like this:

Sarah: "I am divorced and have three kids. I want to get some help for my ex-husband who has an anger problem."

Therapist: "Yes, you have the right man. That's what I do."

Sarah: "My therapist suggested I call you because she thought that you could help him understand that he needs to leave me alone."

Therapist: "So, you've decided that you don't want to reconcile with him and he seems to be having a hard time getting it?"

Sarah: "That's right. I was wondering if I could set up an appointment for us to meet together at your office."

Therapist: "I'm sure that will be fine, but let me ask you a question. What have you done to make it clear to him that you don't want to get back together with him?"

Sarah: "Well, I've had him arrested several times. He spent four months in jail the last time."

Therapist: "What did he do?"

Sarah: "He held me captive at gunpoint in my own house for four days. That was the last episode."

Therapist: "Well, what would be your goal for this session? What would be a good outcome?"

Sarah: "That he would leave me and the kids alone so we could go on with our own lives."

Therapist: "Well, given how he has terrorized you and your kids, I wonder if you have ever fantasized that an even better outcome would be that he have a heart attack and die in the session?"

Sarah: "Oh, yeah. Sometimes I have allowed myself to think that would be the best outcome of all."

Therapist: "Lady, it sounds like you need a lawyer, not a therapist."

Sarah: "I have a lawyer. He says I need a gun, not a lawyer. I wouldn't know how to explain to the children that I killed their father. I just want him to die of natural causes."

Therapist: "I don't see how my meeting with the both of you would do any good. If four months in the county jail hasn't convinced him, I don't think your explaining it to him in my office will do the trick."

Sarah: "So you don't think you can help me?"

Therapist: "Given what you've told me, the only idea that makes sense to me is to send him to prison. I don't see how counseling outside the prison walls is going to help anything." (I felt it would be dangerous and unethical for me to meet with them in my office.)

There are some men who are not going to be amenable to training by their wives or to attend counseling on an outpatient basis. They do need help and some of them can change, but if threatening to leave them or actually leaving them has not gotten their attention to the point that they are running to therapy, then have them arrested and if that doesn't work, it is time for a divorce and a restraining order.

Types of Batterers

The early work on domestic violence, like Lenore Walker's *The Battered Woman*,[36] did not differentiate between different types of batterers. Instead, it focused on the three-stage cycle of family violence. The first stage, tension-building, is typified by "minor" outbursts like throwing things, increased verbal abuse, and increased feelings of fear. The second stage is the actual battering incident. The third stage is kindness and contrite, loving behavior. This stage is marked by apologies, tears, begging for forgiveness and lots of promises about future behavior. The assumption was that all male battering fit this three-stage pattern.

Later research has differentiated between various types of abusive men and their patterns of behavior. Neil Jacobson and John Gottman, both professors at the University of Washington, wrote a ground-breaking book, *When Men Batter Women*. Based on more than 10 years of research with over 200 couples in dangerous relationships, the authors shatter the myth that all batterers are alike.[37]

In conducting their study, Jacobson and Gottman videotaped and observed nonviolent arguments of severe batterers and their spouses, and used control groups of nonviolent yet unhappily married couples. They eliminated much of the subjectivity in analyzing these abusive encounters by hooking up arguing couples to monitors that measured vital signs, such as heart rate and sweat flow. Based on this study, the authors made a number of important new discoveries, including the identification of two types of batterers. *Pit Bulls*, as they call one group, are violent because they are incredibly insecure and have an unhealthy dependence on the mates they abuse. They fear losing their wives and therefore attempt to control them through physical and emotional abuse.

> Pit Bulls are more likely to lose control, letting their emotions burn slowly until they explode in anger. They also tend to become stalkers, unable to let go of relationships that have ended.

Cobras are like the snake for which they are named. They become still and focused just before striking their victim. The more violent of the two, Cobras strike swiftly and ferociously, always remaining in control and feeling entitled to whatever they want, whenever they want it. Cobras have often been physically or sexually abused themselves, frequently in childhood, and tend to see violence as an unavoidable part of life.

> Cobras are cool and methodical as they inflict pain and humiliation on their spouse or lover.

Jacobson and Gottman made another chilling discovery. Unlike Pit Bulls, whose heart rates increase while verbally abusing their wives, the heart rates of Cobras actually decrease during violent arguments. According to their findings:

> Cobras appear to be criminal types who have engaged in anti-social behavior since adolescence. They are hedonistic and impulsive. They beat their wives and abuse them emotionally, to stop them from interfering with the Cobras' need to get what they want when they want it.

> Their wives fear them and are often quite depressed. But fear and depression do not completely explain why the women are unlikely to leave the relationship. Nor is it simply that they lack economic and other resources. Indeed, Cobras are often economically dependent on their wives. Despite the fact that they are being severely abused, it is often the women rather than the men who continue to fight for the continuance of the relationship.[38]

Knowing what type of abuser you are dealing with can be a crucial factor in deciding whether to try to salvage an abusive relationship or whether just to get out for good.

> If you are married to a Cobra, then don't worry about getting him into therapy. Get yourself into therapy and stay there until you discover the tie that is holding you in such a relationship.

John and Nancy were an attractive middle-class couple in their 20s. John was often verbally and physically abusive to Nancy, complete with pushing, shoving and holding her down. Even though I saw them as a couple, I gave Nancy this advice in front of John: "I have never seen a guy who needs a ride downtown in a police car more than he does. This guy needs to be cuffed in his

*jogging shorts and taken to the police car with no shoes or shirt
and with all the neighbors looking. After you get the red lights
flashing in front of your house, then he might be ready for therapy."*

*Nancy was not prepared to use her power in that way since they
were newly married. Erroneously, she believed that the stress
would lessen in time and the problem would go away. About six
months later I got paged on a Friday evening. John was crying
and said that he had gotten divorce papers just a few hours
before. Nancy had changed the locks and gotten a restraining
order. He wanted an appointment as soon as possible, in hopes
that coming to see me would prove to her that he was willing to
change. He saw me for a few months, then he started slipping
again. I again told Nancy that I thought he could make the necessary changes but that he needed the experience of spending a
night in jail and being on probation before he would be able to
make a more permanent change. She pulled the plug and ended
the marriage.*

> Pit Bulls can be inspired to make permanent changes
> when they are threatened with separation, filed on or
> are arrested and put on probation. I encourage women
> to take one of those actions. If he changes, that's good.
> But if he doesn't, go on to the next step.

How can you protect yourself?

Never underestimate the inherent risk or danger involved in an
abusive relationship. Never hold back on pressing charges or calling
911 if there is a threat of physical violence against you or your family. Never. Even if you decide you want to work it out. If he is on
probation, then he knows that he doesn't have much room for slips.

> The most important rule to remember is that if you feel
> threatened, you probably are. Take all threats seriously
> and trust your instincts.

We live in a world where everything is becoming "psychologized." This mental health model is also being used in family violence. Women who have lived under the umbrella of violence and verbal abuse for years are frequently diagnosed as being dependent; having low self-esteem; being codependent or helpless; or being unhealed survivors of sexual abuse. They are, of course, being unfairly compared to nonvictimized women since these labels are ascribed only after women have been abused. Which of us would not have similar symptoms after living for years in an abusive relationship?

Male batterers are also grist for the mental health mill. Insight therapy tries to help angry men understand how they have been affected by their past so that they can respond more appropriately to current relationships. Increased self-esteem is the treatment goal. This therapy is based on creating a nonthreatening atmosphere for the client. But, unlike dealing with simple neurosis like the fear of flying, there is an immediacy to family violence and abuse. Taking the time to create a safe environment for the batterer means continuing the dangerous environment for the partner.

Ventilation models—where men are taught to ventilate their anger—are the most counterproductive. The last thing a rageaholic needs is a therapist's permission to ventilate his anger. A psychotherapeutic intervention may inadvertently increase the risk to the abused woman by missing the most important point: Victims of abuse need to protect themselves and be protected by the law.

> While a murderer may have deep psychological forces driving him, the end result is still a dead victim. All the insight and change that a murderer can muster will not bring the victim back.

The law offers women and families important protection. One example is the Violence Against Women Act (VAWA)[39] passed by Congress in 1994. VAWA is targeted primarily at domestic violence and sexual assault and was designed to improve the response of police, prosecutors and judges to crimes against women. It was also designed to increase funding for battered women's shelters. Among other things, VAWA guarantees that protection orders entered into any court will be enforced nationwide. It also provides penalties for crossing state lines to abuse a spouse or violate a protection order. The act prohibits anyone facing a restraining order for domestic abuse from possessing a firearm. In 1998 another initiative was passed that allows threatened women to obtain new Social Security numbers more easily. Women can now move, get new jobs, open bank accounts, and start over without fear that abusers will hunt them down by tracking their Social Security numbers.

In addition to the protection offered by VAWA, many municipalities have a pro-arrest policy whereby police are required to arrest someone when answering a domestic abuse call. Most cities and many rural areas have shelters for battered and abused women. Additional resources for battered women are found at the end of this chapter.

Not all batterers are alike, nor is the progression of their violence always predictable. Psychotherapists try to be realistic about the extent of people's ability to change. While most angry men may be capable of changing, this change may come too late or it may not be enough. In the case of Cobras, change may not even be possible. If you are living with a Cobra or a ferocious Pit Bull, you need to figure out how to get yourself out of a dangerous relationship. While therapy can provide insight and support, it cannot provide physical protection. Moreover, most battered women quickly learn the limitations of the police and judicial systems.

If you want to leave an abusive relationship, you must create a safety plan. As part of that plan, you need to know where you can get help and how to keep yourself safe. This escape plan should include everything from mental preparation to financial records, to toll-free numbers for rental cars and hotel rooms, to phone numbers and addresses of battered women's shelters. You should also know what steps to take during the actual move, how to secure your home after leaving, how to navigate the legal system, how to ensure the safety of your children and how to defend against stalking. Lastly, you need to know what rights you have once the police are called and how later to use the courts for protection. Abused women can regain control of their lives in the same way that rageaholic men must learn to take charge of their behavior.

RESOURCES FOR BATTERED WOMEN

Organizations

* National Domestic Violence Hotline
  Phone: (800) 799-SAFE (7233)
  Phone (TTY): (800) 787-3224
  PO Box 161810
  Austin, TX 78716
  Web site: http://www.ndvh.org/

* National Coalition Against Domestic Violence
  Phone: (303) 839-1852
  Fax: (303) 831-9251
  1201 E. Colfax Ave. Suite #385
  PO Box 18749
  Denver, CO 80218-0749
  Web site: http://www.ncadv.org

* National Clearinghouse for the Defense of Battered Women
  Phone: (215) 351-0010
  125 S. 9th Street Suite #302
  Philadelphia, PA 19107

* Center for the Protection Against Sexual and Domestic Violence
  936 N 34th Street, Suite 200
  Seattle, WA 98103
  Phone: (206) 634-1903
  Fax (206) 634-0115
  Web site: http://www.cpsdv.org/

* Silent Witness
  Phone: (612) 623-0999
  Fax: (612) 623-0999
  20 2nd Street NE, Suite #1101
  Minneapolis, MN 55413
  Web site: http://www.silentwitness.net/

Books and Articles

Berry, Dawn. (1998). *The Domestic Violence Sourcebook: Everything You Need to Know.* Los Angeles, CA: Lowell House.

Betancourt, Marian. (1997). *What to Do When Love Turns Violent: A Practical Resource for Women in Abusive Relationships.* New York, NY: Harper Perennial Library.

Jacobson, Neil & Gottman, John. (1998). *When Men Batter Women: New Insights into Ending Abusive Relationships.* New York, NY: Simon & Schuster.

Moltz, D. (1992), "Abuse and Violence: The Dark Side of the Family," *Journal of Marriage and Family Therapy,* pp. 223-230.

Murphy-Milano, Susan. (1996). *Defending Our Lives: Getting Away from Domestic Violence and Staying Safe.* Landover Hills, MD: Anchor Books.

CHAPTER 5

HOW TO GET A PIT BULL'S ATTENTION AND MAKE HIM BEHAVE

If you are clear that you have a Pit Bull and not a Cobra, then how do you get the Pit Bull's attention in a way that will put him in the mood to learn? First, you have to learn what scares a Pit Bull more than anything else. Most Pit Bulls are terrified of separation. Often the threat of separation alone will bring them to their knees. This is the number one way to get a Pit Bull's attention. It worked on me. Eighty percent of the angry men I see come to my office after their wives tell them, "Either you get into one of Hightower's groups or I am out of here."

The first method in getting a Pit Bull's attention is to threaten to leave him and then point him in the direction of a good therapist, counselor or relationship coach who can get him on the right path. Secondly, when you send him off to therapy, be clear about what behaviors he needs to change. You might send along a copy of this book with the instruction to stop some or all of the key dysfunctional behaviors discussed earlier. Also, demand that the Pit Bull start speaking to you like it says to do in this book. Do not send him off to a therapist with an agenda to work on some childhood problem. Let him and his therapist figure out how best to accomplish the goal of stopping the expression of anger.

> Be clear on the behavior(s) you want stopped and what behavior(s) you want started. Your needs, desires and wants count.

Wives who have been in therapy for a while are often much too lenient in their expectations of change. In fact, psychotherapists married to rageful men are frequently the worst in terms of being overtolerant of rageful behavior.

I had a couple (Rosa and Ralph) in therapy. Both were therapists. Ralph had a bad rage problem. At the end of the first session the dialogue went like this:

Rosa: "I know I can't expect him to change overnight. It took him 35 years to get this way. It may take years to get to the root of his anger problem."

Therapist: "Let me be clear about something. He never, ever, ever has to rage again for the rest of his life. He now knows what to do to prevent rage outbursts. Don't ever let him off the hook again. Never excuse any rage eruption he has toward you or anyone else."

Rosa: "But I know that real change takes time."

Therapist: "Yes, and it starts right now. He never, ever has to blow up at you or anyone else again, regardless of his childhood traumas and his relationship with his mother."

Rosa: "But he has deep underlying issues with his father."

Therapist: "That may be true and it may take a long time to work them out. In the meantime, he doesn't ever have to blow up again. He now has the tools to stop it."

Rosa: "You make it sound like he can change in one session."

Therapist: "He can change with no sessions. Psychotherapy or coaching can help, but I have worked with men who have made a complete transformation before they ever saw me. They had stopped their angry behaviors. They changed the way they spoke to their wives. One also knew that he had to forgive his father for the abuse he received before he could become a good husband and father. I have that man on videotape at his first psychotherapy session. I show it to therapists when I do training to illustrate my point."

Not only can these angry men change, they can change immediately. Not only can they change immediately, but they can change permanently. Not only can they change immediately and permanently, but they can do it without psychotherapy.

I can say all that because I have seen it over and over again. Also, because it was true for me. The last time I called my wife any kind of derogatory name was nine years ago while driving around the park in our little Mazda RX-7. From that day forward, I never called her another name. That fateful day broke a 30-year pattern of name-calling. For the 30 years before that, I called every woman I had ever been intimately involved with names when I was angry. All this name-calling went on while I was in therapy working on my "underlying problems." Have I been furious with my wife on occasion since then? Of course. But I haven't called her names.

Once you get your man to therapy, make sure he doesn't use it as an excuse not to change. I did that for many years. An incident with my wife almost 10 years ago illustrates how "sneaky guys" can use therapy as an excuse. Although I've forgotten the context of the argument, I had lost my temper a few hours before and was in the apology stage.

Wife: "I'm tired of your apologies. Three weeks later you go back and do the same thing."

Newton: "You are right. I am going to go back into therapy to work on some unresolved family of origin issues and really get to the root of things this time."

Wife: "What about the consequences of blowing up? What do you think they should be?"

Newton: "I just said that I was willing to go back to therapy and work on underlying and painful family of origin issues."

Wife: "No. You are missing the point. I was thinking more like cleaning out the cat box for the next month. Also, to probate your sentence, if you have any kind of a slip-up, we can add the toilets. Then if you slip again, you can take over all my household chores. That is what I mean by consequences."

Newton: "Okay. You write it up and I will sign it."

(After three weeks I was doing all the household chores around the house.)

Wife: "Hey, this worked out great. I'm ready for you to have another tantrum any time."

> You know you are on the right track when you look forward to him having a good temper tantrum, and he is terrified of blowing up again. When that happens, you know that you have gotten your Pit Bull's attention.

One reason that a Pit Bull acts the way he does is that he finds the consequences of his anger outbursts tolerable or even rewarding. For example, my suggestion that the "punishment" for my anger outburst should be to go back into therapy was rewarding for me. I could go into therapy and have someone who would unconditionally listen to me for an hour. I'd get some solid focused attention. Not a good consequence for an anger outburst.

To some degree, children misbehave because they are allowed to. This is reinforced when they find the punishment for their misbehavior tolerable. For example, "Johnny, you misbehaved; now go to your room without dinner." That may be a tolerable consequence if Johnny had already eaten 40 cookies since he arrived home and has a TV set in his room. Rageaholics need to have consequences for their behaviors that they find unpleasant. This may include being humiliated in front of neighbors as they are handcuffed and driven in a police car downtown, spending the night in jail, paying a fine, losing their job, being separated from their partner, or having sex or affection withheld.

> The way to get a Pit Bull's attention is to make sure that the consequences of his behavior are unpleasant for him.

Now that you have his attention, make him behave.

If you are married to a rager, I suggest you develop a contract with him (not *on* him). The first part of the contract should state that if you feel he is getting angry during a discussion, one of you should take a time-out.

A time-out is simple. You or the rageaholic stops speaking and then quietly leaves the room. That means that neither of you slams the door or curses when you leave. You or your partner comes back within an hour. If you are in a therapy session and you leave the room, come back when you feel you can contain yourself. Often when I see angry couples together, my office has a revolving door. One gets up and leaves, and then that person comes back and the other leaves. One ground rule is that yelling is not permitted in the therapy session. If you get angry, rather than explode, practice leaving. It's not a sign of failure; it's a sign of good work. This is one of my ground rules for therapy. It should also be one of the ground rules for your marriage.

The second part of the contract should state that when you interrupt the rager, he must let you speak. Otherwise, you will be like me in the days before I knew how to work with ragers. I would see ragers individually and they would talk on and on. They liked it, but they didn't get better.

They came to the therapy session and bragged to me that, "I told him this and I told him that...and then I told him that I wasn't going to take that anymore." Since I couldn't interrupt him, all I could do was listen to his hero stories about how he told someone off. That's what I call helping him get two rushes for the price of one. The rageaholic gets the anger rush when he gets mad at the person and then gets a second anger rush when retelling the story.

If you are a therapist reading this, you know that your work does make a difference. As a helping professional, you can either put gasoline or water on the fires of the rageful man. There are definite water techniques and there are definite gasoline techniques. Some domestic violence writers suggest that people with rage and violence problems can't change. I proved years ago they can by making them worse. It's not hard if you use gasoline tactics like encouraging them to express their anger.

> There can be dramatic changes for angry men. These changes can happen quickly and they can even happen without psychotherapy. On the other hand, psychotherapy can make some of the angry behaviors worse, especially if it allows the rageaholic to rage in the therapy session.

How do you make the rager behave? First, you must make it clear that you will not tolerate his behavior. In some cases, threats will suffice while in other cases you will have to act decisively by filing divorce or separation papers or by getting a restraining order. Many Pit Bulls will not go into therapy willingly. Some will consider therapy only when faced with the prospect of losing what is most valuable to them, usually their wife and family. Others will need to be ordered by the court to attend therapy sessions.

As mentioned earlier, you must create consequences for the rageaholic's behavior that he finds unpleasant. These consequences will differ among men. For some men, unpleasant consequences will be emotional, for others financial; for still others it will involve the public humiliation of being arrested. In other words, you have to find a consequence that affects the rager.

There are no guarantees, but you can increase your odds.

Many people believe in the Protestant work ethic of love and intimacy. If you just work hard enough, the relationship will work. If the relationship fails, it means that you haven't worked at it enough. Even though you and your partner work hard and even though your partner may have controlled his rage, there are no guarantees that the marriage will work. Nor are there guarantees that both of you will decide to stay in the marriage. Anger problems frequently mask other issues. When the anger problem is extinguished, the other problems may surface. Even though your rageaholic makes all the right moves, you may still decide to leave.

Take, for example, the case of Sam and Carolyn. Although Sam had apparently done everything Carolyn had asked, she still wanted a separation.

Therapist: "Carolyn, I believe it is possible for you to have a happy marriage with Sam. I believe you have his attention like never before. You have done the work that I know took many years to do. You have had the courage to say, 'Hey, this is not working for me.' Now, thanks to your assertive skills and willingness to draw boundaries and set limits, I believe there really is a way to inspire Sam to be more loving, to become more involved with the kids, to stop drinking and to make you the number one priority in his life. I know that it is imperative for Sam to change."

Carolyn: "I don't know if Sam is capable of doing that."

Sam: "Carolyn, I know you would like me to compliment you more, to be more affectionate without it leading to sex, to be more honest about what I'm doing and to share more of what's going on inside of me, like my joys, fears and victories of the day."

Carolyn: "You have not done that for many years and it has left a real void in me. I don't know if you can ever fill that void again. You have so many deep-seated problems."

Therapist: "Sometimes the more we know about the causes of relationship problems, the more confused we get on how to improve things. Knowing that Sam could be an alcoholic, a workaholic, a sex addict and a rageaholic did not necessarily lead to knowing what to do to get him to change his behavior. However, you did know what to do."

Carolyn: "It took a lot of strength and willpower."

Therapist: "You've done an excellent job in starting the change process and moving your marriage forward in a positive direction. First, you got him to marital therapy with someone who was an expert in recovery issues. Next, you convinced him to go through the program at the Center for Recovering Families. Next, you encouraged him to follow through on the referral made to me. I suggested and encouraged Sam to go to an AA meeting and to join a men's group. You supported both of these things and he's doing them. You need to give yourself some credit for doing many things that will lead you to a more fulfilling marriage.

"You've also done an excellent job of diagnosing Sam's problems. You've broken through your timidity and made it clear what you wanted him to do. You have also put enough pressure on him to do it. I commend you for this. In fact, you could give lessons to most of my clients' wives.

"Very few men I work with are happy to accept their wife's diagnosis of them as an alcoholic, workaholic, sex addict, rageaholic, narcissistic, controlling, self-centered, self-absorbed jerk. Especially when it is true. There are usually a few months of resentment following such an accurate assessment."

Sam: "Very few people, including myself, would respond to this kind of confrontation with, 'Honey, thank you for sharing. You are absolutely right. I will get to work on myself right away.' Most men are probably like me. They would be defensive and counterattack."

Therapist: (to Carolyn) "Your strategies up until now have been well thought out and well executed. The proof is in the pudding. The change process is under way and picking up momentum. Now that change is happening, it may be important that it not happen too quickly and to make sure that it is going in a positive direction for you, Sam and the kids. It may also be getting close to a point where you might want to try some other tactics. Some strategies may simply work better than others at this point."

Sam: "It may also be time to explore strategies that don't leave me feeling so coerced. If you did that, I might be more responsive and accommodating."

Therapist: (to Carolyn) "I believe that you can create the kind of relationship you've always wanted. You can rekindle the love you felt when you first met Sam. You can get Sam to be more communicative and involved. You can get him to be more sensitive to your feelings. This process may have already started."

Carolyn: "But then why is there more distance between us now than before? Why am I no closer to having joy in my life than when we started therapy and Sam made all those changes? Sometimes I think that the only way I'll ever get the kind of fulfillment I need is to trade him in for someone new."

Therapist: (to Carolyn) "You may be right, but I have found that trade-ins are not very practical. New men need relationship training too. That's why I am hoping that you'll keep him around for a while and transform him into the 'new and improved' version you've been hoping for.

"I know both of you have spent a lot of years in traditional psychoanalytically oriented therapy. I know that traditional therapists believe that the key to resolving problems in your life lies in understanding the forces in your childhood. In theory, once you recognize how the past has influenced you, you'll know why you do what you do and your problems will disappear. There is a lot of truth in this and many people find it very effective. However, you probably know someone who has great insight into his childhood and recognizes why he overeats, yet he continues to raid the refrigerator night after night.

"Perhaps it's time to experiment with a new approach for a short time. Perhaps it's time to start identifying how you both want to change your lives separately and together, then get clear on the steps needed to make that happen. I see that you have already begun to do this with all the changes you have instigated in the last several months. You are living proof that one person can change a relationship single-handedly, no matter what the books say. Incidentally, I agree with you. I can't tell you how many marriages I've seen rebuilt when the person most interested in making things better stopped pointing fingers and started taking productive action, like you have. Time and time again, I've observed relationships having near-death experiences resurrected by the one determined person who was willing to tip over the first domino."

Carolyn: "In Alanon, I have always heard that the only person I can change is myself. I can't change other people."

Therapist: "You are proof that it's not true; otherwise how do you think Sam ended up in an AA meeting? I believe you can certainly change other people, but—and here's the big 'but'—you must begin by changing your own actions first. Relationships are such that if one person changes, the other person must change as well. You might think of what would happen if you got tired of playing tennis with Sam and the next time you went to the tennis court you brought a baseball and glove. There is no way he can play tennis with you without your cooperation...and that takes a tennis racket. The way I reconcile this Alanon slogan is, 'If I invest too much time in changing other people and I think they have to change for me to be happy, it is a way for me to avoid looking inside myself. I am then into my co-dependency. If I spend too much time explaining to people why they should change, instead of spelling out the changes I want, then I am again into my co-dependency.'"

Focus on taking effective action to bring about change rather than just complaining and explaining.

Why Rats Are Smarter Than People

One of the biggest mistakes I see my clients make repeatedly when working on their relationship problems is to do what "feels right" whether it works or not. Rats don't make that mistake, which is why they are smarter than people.

If you put a rat at the bottom of a maze in front of five tunnels and you put cheese in one of these tunnels, the rat will explore all the tunnels, looking for the cheese. If you put the cheese down tunnel five each time you do the experiment, eventually the rat will remember that the cheese is down tunnel five and go there first each time. In other words, the rat will stop looking for the cheese in the other four tunnels.

If you then decide to put the cheese down the second tunnel, the rat will go up the fifth tunnel, notice there's no cheese and then go back down. The rat may do this two or three more times, but it will soon figure out that the cheese is no longer there and start exploring the other tunnels until it again finds the cheese. The major difference between rats and humans is that rats will stop going up tunnels that have no cheese. Some people will go up the fifth tunnel forever. They will spend months, even years, going down empty relationship tunnels even if they are in pain because, unlike the rat who is just focused on the prize, they lose sight of why they are doing what they are doing. They forget that the goal is to have a happy, loving relationship.

> **Sam:** (to Carolyn after therapist's rat story) "Maybe it's time to use a little cheese when I go down the right tunnel. I also need you to keep your hand on the switch to provide a shock when I go down the wrong tunnel."

> **Therapist:** (to Carolyn) "It's great that you have found your voice to tell Sam when he's doing things you don't like. It may also be useful to tell him when he's doing something right and smile (a big reinforcer for most of us). This doesn't mean that you have to compromise your boundaries or that you should believe everything is now all right. The emphasis on positive reinforcement may be a skill that hasn't worked before, but it may work in the new context you have created.

"Using both negative and positive reinforcers around your boundaries may increase your effectiveness. Keep sharing your negative feelings, but also stop censoring your positive ones if you happen to have one or two. Maybe catch Sam in the act of doing what you want him to do and reward him in some way. This doesn't mean completely forgiving him before you are ready or that you should trust him completely."

Carolyn: "Sam will have to earn back my trust over time. I can't make myself vulnerable to him until I feel safe."

Therapist: "I'm not talking about the 'big' things. I'm talking about something simple like a compliment without a 'but,' a hug or a short note."

Carolyn: "It's important for me to stop stuffing my feelings and to continue my development as a strong-willed, independent woman. It's vital for me to have my voice heard."

Therapist: "You've made enormous progress in dealing with a strong, controlling man. You certainly have the upper hand now. Sam wants me to help him make you happy and not be so self-absorbed with his own needs and wants. It would be great if you could point out to him if he accidentally does this."

Sam: "I thought that two of the big impasses in our marriage were that I was not in regular therapy and would not go to AA meetings. Now that I've done both of these things, why do you want a separation? I'm confused."

Carolyn: "Sam, I still love you, but I'm not sure that the changes you've made aren't too little and too late. I don't know if those changes alone are enough to make me happy in this relationship."

Even though a couple does the right things (e.g., follows the steps in this book and goes into marital therapy, support groups, etc.), there is no guarantee that a relationship will work. There is also no guarantee that after the husband changes he will still want to be in the relationship. Because you have dragged him into therapy and encouraged him to change also does not mean that you are committing yourself to a lifetime with your partner.

Michele Weiner-Davis, in her book *How to Change Your Man*, sums up the predicament for Sam and many other men:

> Despite my best efforts, some relationships have fallen through the cracks. Although this, in and of itself, is not particularly remarkable, what is remarkable is the definite pattern I noticed; it is primarily women that are walking out of their marriages. In fact, a journalist recently coined the phrase "Walkaway Wives." Here's the behind-the-scenes look at what the Walkaway Wife syndrome is all about.
>
> After years of trying unsuccessfully to improve an unhappy marriage, a woman eventually surrenders and convinces herself that change isn't possible. She ends up believing there's absolutely nothing she can do to influence her partner to be more responsive, so she carefully maps out the logistics of what she considers to be the inevitable—getting a divorce.
>
> While she's planning her escape, she no longer tries to improve her relationship or modify her partner's behavior in any way. She resigns herself to living in silent desperation until "D Day." Unfortunately, her husband views his wife's silence as an indication that "everything is fine." After all, the "nagging" has ceased. That's why, when she finally breaks the news of the impending divorce, her shell-shocked partner replies, "I had no idea you were unhappy." This response serves as further evidence of her husband's unfathomable insensitivity to her feelings, and the decision to dissolve their relationship becomes etched in stone. Even when her husband undergoes real and lasting changes, it's usually too late. The same impenetrable wall that for years shielded her from pain now prevents her from truly recognizing his genuine willingness to change. The relationship is over.[40]

In the process of a partner's change, you will also change. No one can know for sure where the journey will lead a couple, but it is worth the risk for most of us.

SECTION III:

THE NEW ABCS FOR WOMEN WHO ARE TRAINING ANGRY MEN

"Pain and suffering are inevitable; being miserable is optional."
—Art Clanin

CHAPTER 6

A = ABSTAIN

ABSTAIN FROM THESE BEHAVIORS AND PHRASES

Just as angry men need to abstain from saying certain phrases, so do their wives. Some of the things wives say to their raging spouses inflame the situation, much like throwing gasoline on a fire that is burning out of control. Other times they use phrases that let the rager off the hook too easily without insisting he take responsibility for what he has done. Other phrases make it too easy for the rager to avoid committing to doing something real to make amends for his behavior.

"How do I know if he is a real rageaholic?"

I worried when Betty came into my office by herself and said she wanted to find out if her husband had a real rage problem. I wanted to say, "It's the wrong question." Instead, I asked her:

Therapist: "Betty, if we knew the answer to that, how would that be helpful?'"

Betty: "Well, if I knew for sure he was, then maybe I could tell him to get help. I worry that it's me."

Therapist: "What's he doing that you would like for him to stop?"

Betty: "He yells at the children, is sarcastic and critical of me all the time."

Therapist: "Is that what you would like to see changed?"

Betty: "Yes."

Therapist: "What have you tried?"

Betty: "I keep explaining to him that it is not good for the children to hear him put me down and call me names all the time."

Therapist: "It does sound like he is a rager: he yells, screams, is sarcastic and calls you names. The problem is that I don't think explaining that to him is going to make any difference. Betty, I think you need to eat your psychological Wheaties™ so you can stand up to this guy and get him to come see me. After you go to therapy and are able to stand up to him, then come back and see me and we will get him in here."

Betty: "I thought you were going to tell me something to help him."

Therapist: "I could, but I don't think you are quite up to it yet. Maybe I am wrong. Are you ready to file for divorce, get a restraining order on him and have the locks changed?"

Betty: "I am shocked. How would that be helpful to him?"

Therapist: "It might get him in the mood to call me when you hand him my card."

Betty: "Isn't there somewhere I can get him some help?"

Therapist: "Has he ever slapped you or pushed you?"

Betty: "Only a few times. The last was last week."

Therapist: "Well, you need to take down this number—911. If he ever puts a hand on you again in anger call it. The research shows that a night in jail works much better than six counseling sessions. Of course, both is the best choice. It sounds like your husband needs pre-therapy treatment."

Betty: "I'm afraid to ask, but what is that?"

Therapist: "A ride downtown in the police car. That often gets men in the mood for counseling about their anger problem."

Betty: "I couldn't do that. Are you saying that you can't help him?"

Therapist: "No. I think I can help him change, but you must provide the motivation and I will provide the therapy. That's the deal."

Betty: "Who could I see to get my psychological Wheaties™?"

Therapist: "I will give you a name of a person who specializes in Wheaties™."

Abstain from the following comments:

1. "Go ahead and tell me how you really feel."

We rageaholics love to tell you how we really feel. Sometimes a statement like, "Go ahead and tell me how you really feel" is all we need to have a good tantrum. If he is working in the program outlined in Section II, then he is going to be working very hard not to tell you how he really feels, if that feeling is anger. Something better might be to wait a day and say: "It looked like you were a little annoyed with me last night. Thank you for controlling yourself. I really appreciate it."

2. "Tell me when you are angry. Don't let it build up."

The idea is for him never to use the "A" word again. It would be great if he could learn to talk about all his other feelings, but he doesn't need to tell you when he is angry. Wives and girlfriends worry when they see the anger building up in their rageaholic. They often have a feeling that if he would get it out in a hurry, then there wouldn't be so much of the anger when it finally comes out. Just because it builds up doesn't mean that he has to let it out. He can keep the lid on the pressure cooker and just let it dissolve.

3. "We need to resolve this right NOW!"

The research shows that 80 percent of the time, couples resolve their problems when each partner understands the other person's point of view. We often use the phrase "resolving it" to mean we are going to decide who is right about this and that, of course, is me. Seldom does that form of "resolving it" lead to problem resolution. Communicating with a rageaholic often means discussing things in 10-minute segments. First, have him focus on listening to you and mirroring back what you say for 10 minutes. Then, the next night, you can do the same for him. Or the two of you can generate different solutions without evaluating them. One person can be the secretary and write them down. The next night the two of you can come back to the possibilities and discuss each one. "If you are not too upset, could you share your feelings with me in a soft voice and I will mirror them back for 10 minutes to see if I understand where you are coming from on this issue? If we are successful, then you can listen to me tomorrow night."

4. "You are always running away. You never want to talk with me."

The rageaholic needs to leave when his temper is about to blow. Sometimes if you are complaining about him or talking about what he perceives as an insoluble problem, then he may feel he cannot take it anymore and needs to get out of the room. Some men need "chit chat" lessons so they can have a little conversation that will please their wife in the evening. However, most of us do not want to be chewed out and if it keeps going on, then leaving the room is the best thing for him to do. If he gets up to leave, you may try saying, "Honey, I am sorry I went on and on about the gutters needing cleaning. You are a wonderful husband. Thank you for all you do. Now come back and sit on the couch and talk to me. I promise not to complain anymore tonight."

5. "If you are going to scream at me, then I am going to scream at you."

This is a surefire way to escalate the problem. I can assure you that you won't teach him a lesson and that he is not going to stop screaming forever after this yelling match.

When he starts to raise his voice, then say, "Please lower your voice." If he is following the recommendations proposed earlier in this book, then he will say, "I'm sorry. Thank you for pointing it out." If he starts to raise his voice again, don't be shy about pointing it out to him again in a nice tone. If he gets too loud, then simply say, "I am not going to talk with you when you are yelling at me."

6. "You are sick and you will never get better. Men like you only get worse over time."

This is certainly true of some batterers. My point here is that it is not a very helpful thing to say to a man, especially if you want him to get counseling for his problem. If you see him as a batterer who is only getting worse over time, then leave. Don't stick around and tell him about it. Whether it is true or not, there is no value in saying it.

When things calm down, you may want to say, "Honey, you are going to have to get some help with that temper of yours. Would you like for me to ask my counselor who might be good for you to see?" This is a first approach. A later approach might be to ask for a "therapeutic separation" to work on the problem with the goal of getting back together after ninety days. There is no dating of other people during the separation.

7. "How can you say you love me when you treat me like that?"

Absolutely true. It makes no sense. This statement will provoke his declaration of undying, eternal love, which will likely hook you back into the relationship without anything changing. It is completely irrelevant whether he feels like he loves you or not. He needs to change the way he talks and acts. That is the point. Love is not the subject.

A conversation about love shouldn't be happening. Rather you should be talking to him the next day from work after spending the night in a Motel 6. Your question to him should be, "I believe you love me. That is not the problem. The problem is what you are you going to *do* differently so I don't have to divorce you. You said that you would stop cursing. You have not done that. What are you willing to do to make this up to me? How about you not taking a vacation, but giving me your vacation pay? My sister and I will use it to go to Hawaii."

8. "Go ahead and hit me. I know that's what you really want to do."

This has to be one of the worst ones. Perhaps women say this to prove they are not afraid and to protest against being controlled and intimidated. No matter what the motivation, don't say it. Instead practice "silence." Silence is one of the most powerful of all responses; it is certainly more productive than saying "hit me."

9. "You're crazy. The things you get jealous over make no sense at all."

Many men with anger problems also have problems with jealousy. Men often know that what they are jealous about is irrational because it doesn't even make sense to them. They often feel crazy and have to go through some pretty convoluted reasoning to explain why their feelings are justified. We jealous, rageful men often feel we are crazy at those moments. Calling men "crazy" often confirms their worst fear. The breakthrough for me happened when my wife said, "I know it is horrible to feel jealous. I hate that feeling myself. I know you don't want to feel that way. What can I do to help you get over it?"

I then uttered a phrase I had never said before, "I need reassurance."

I have taught these simple sentences to couples who have had jealousy problems for years. The argument over whether you were flirting or he is crazy is useless. The two of you can get over this one easier than you think. Give the man some reassurance that "you are the only man for me and I love you."

10. "THIS IS IT. I am going to divorce you this time. No one is going to talk to me like that."

Threatening divorce during an argument is never good. Angry men are often the biggest babies in the world and the thing they fear the most is being left. This can trigger a bigger tantrum, and the focus changes from his behavior to your leaving. I am *not* saying that separating is not a good idea. Sometimes getting a divorce *is* a good idea, but *threatening* divorce is *not* a good idea in the middle of an argument. This is a good time for a time-out. When he has cooled down, then you can say, "That was horrible the way you talked to me. What are you going to do to make it up to me?" If the kids heard it, then he needs to apologize to you in front of the kids and explain to them that what he did was wrong (no babbling like, "My behavior was inappropriate, but your mother made me mad").

11. "You will never get any better until you go to therapy and work through your issues with your father. That's what my therapist said is wrong with you."

There is almost nothing more infuriating than to hear that your wife's therapist thinks you have deep-seated problems that account for all of your marital difficulties. I believe that couples are headed for trouble when they psychologically diagnose each other and suggest what issues the other needs to work on. I encourage couples to make behavioral requests of each other but not go into "psychology land." Secondly, I believe that men can make an impressive beginning without going back through past trauma. If you want him to get into therapy, it's better to take him along to see your therapist. For instance, "Honey, I know you don't believe in this psychological stuff, but I would really appreciate it if you would go to my next counseling appointment with me."

In Summary...

Abstinence from certain phrases is important for women who love ragers, because it is a beginning of placing effective limits on the rager. The days of arguing, discussing and diagnosing are over. They have not worked. It is time to draw lines in the sand with your words: "This is what I want you to do."

ABSTAIN FROM THESE COMMENTS:

1. "Go ahead and tell me how you really feel."
2. "Tell me when you are angry. Don't let it build up."
3. "We need to resolve this right NOW!"
4. "You are always running away. You never want to talk with me."
5. "If you are going to scream at me, then I am going to scream at you."
6. "You are sick and you will never get better. Men like you only get worse over time."
7. "How can you say you love me when you treat me like that?"
8. "Go ahead and hit me. I know that's what you really want to do."
9. "You're crazy. The things you get jealous over make no sense at all."
10. "THIS IS IT. I am going to divorce you this time. No one is going to talk to me like that."
11. "You will never get any better until you go to therapy and work through your issues with your father. That is what my therapist said is wrong with you."

CHAPTER 7

B = BELIEVE

BELIEFS FOR WOMEN WHO LOVE ANGRY MEN

Introduction

Our beliefs guide our actions. The following beliefs are important for women to be able to say to themselves as they work to change the behaviors of their partners. These beliefs are based on what works to change behavior: 1) Making it absolutely clear what you want; 2) offering praise when the right behavior is evident; and 3) punishing when the wrong behavior appears.

1. "There is nothing wrong with me getting him to change."

It is still amazing to me when I do the initial interview with an angry man and I ask him, "What would your wife want you to do differently so that you would be the man of her dreams?" (Women get ready to cringe.)

The number one answer is, "Make more money."

When I continue to ask the question in different ways, he has some vague answers like "communicate better."

Then I ask him what that means. "What would you be doing if you were to communicate better?" He often has no ideas. At this point, I sometimes call his wife during the session and say, "Your husband has said (which he has) that he loves you very much. He will do anything to keep the marriage together, but I am having a hard time figuring out how he needs to change to please you." I ask her to come with him to make sure we are headed in the right direction when it comes to pleasing her because that is what he wants to learn how to do.

To his shock, her number one answer to what she wants him to do differently to become the man of her dreams is to "listen to me." Then she and I together spell out what that means: 1) Turn off the TV; 2) look at her; 3) repeat back what she says; 4) ask "What else?" and 5) say "Thank you for sharing."

We then practice these things in the session and I ask her to give him a grade. He usually gets an "A." If not, we repeat it until he gets an A. He is thrilled to know what to *do*. If he says, "I don't understand why she wants that," I ask, "Are you here for psychological understanding or to make your wife happy?"

2. "There is nothing wrong with him wanting to change to please me."

There is a difference in therapy for depressed women as opposed to angry men. Depressed women have gone around trying to please others while ignoring their own needs. Therapists who work with depressed women tell them, "Don't change for him. Only change because *you* want to change."

Don't despair when he doesn't want to work on his inner child or work through his issues with his parents. The self-help books you have been reading are for depressed women. He can change and stay changed regardless of his motivation. It is progress for angry men to want to get their attention off of what they want and be willing to change for you. John M. Gottman, a leading researcher in the field of marriage and family therapy, has stated that a husband's willingness to be influenced by his wife is one of the signs that the couple will have a long and happy marriage.[41]

3. "It's better to figure out the solution than to figure out the cause."

First of all, "psychologically diagnosing" him does not help you come up with creative ideas for change. Blaming and complaining are not the catalyst for change in any human relationship.

Secondly, when you tell him what is wrong with him such as, "You are a rageaholic, alcoholic, workaholic, insensitive, self-centered, self-absorbed, narcissistic jerk," odds are he is not going to say, "You know you are right, Honey. I have never thought of it that way." Even if he has read the first part of the book and answers that way, nothing has changed, even though you are right.

4. "There is a better way to change the relationship than 'talking things out.'"

Gottman also found out that happily married couples spend less time sharing their feelings and trying to talk things out than unhappily married couples. Another psychological "truth" of the last 50 years bites the dust under the microscope of scientific research.

According to Michele Weiner-Davis,[42]

"We [women] too frequently assume that men are like us; that they feel relieved after hashing things out in conversation. Actually, men generally do whatever they can to steer clear of lengthy, intimate tete-a-tetes, because they're not as comfortable with talking as we are. It's why men withdraw when women want to talk about relationship issues. It's not because they don't love us or care about our feelings. It's just that it feels unsettling to them. They're out of their domain.

"We can't help but feel offended and hurt. We assume they're not committed to making the relationship work. We assume they're selfish and unloving. Right?

"Look, just because your man is sick of talking, or doesn't seem to hear a word you say, you shouldn't take it to mean that he doesn't care about your feelings. It may just mean that he's gotten word-saturated, and it's time to switch gears."

5. "Love and trust are two separate things."

When I began the session with Jane and Bill, I asked my standard question:

Therapist: "What's better?"

Jane: "Well, actually he is doing great. I have no complaints for the past two months since we saw you

last and he started the group. I wonder though if I
can really trust him."

Therapist: "Absolutely not. Don't trust him."

Bill: "Wait a minute."

Jane: "What do you mean? When should I start trusting
him?"

Therapist: "I believe that you should trust him only as much
as he has earned. Trust should not be given away."

Jane: "But I do love him."

Therapist: "It's important not to get trust and love mixed up.
I learned about this when my daughter went off to
college. She had a less than admirable record handling money at the time. She called and asked if I
would give her a credit card on my account, with
her name on it. I asserted, 'It's not going to happen.' She said, 'You don't trust me.' My response
was she was absolutely right. I did not trust her
with a credit card. She started crying and said, 'You
don't love me.' My reply was that I loved her with
all my heart and would give up my life for her in a
second, but I would not give her a credit card. She
laughed and said, 'Dad, sometimes you don't make
any sense.' I agreed."

Jane: "Should I let him back in the house?"

Therapist: "What would he have to do to prove that he was
ready to come back in the house?"

*Jane worked out what he would need to do and discovered that
he had already done it, but she wanted him to keep it up for
another month before he could move back in.*

6. "I have complete trust in my ability to take action when needed."

Rather than worrying about whether he has changed, it might be
better to ask yourself whether you could now take whatever action
is needed if he slipped again. This could range from asking him to
clean the toilets for a month if he yelled, to going to marital therapy,
separation, filing for divorce or calling the police. Sometimes I suggest that women be given a sizeable savings account in their name

only to increase their security. Other women have asked for all the assets to be divided in a post-nuptial agreement before the man moves back in.

7. "A little psychological pain can be a good thing."

Sometimes a wife is worried because her husband feels so bad about what he said or did. They are often surprised by my response.

Therapist: "Good, he should feel bad. It was an awful thing he did. How is he going to make it up to you?"

Wife: "I'm willing to forgive him. I can see he feels really bad."

Therapist: "Oh, my God. You can't forgive him yet. He has to DO something, not just feel guilty. What do you want? Money, flowers, a trip, yard work, housework?"

Wife: (laughing) "You mean I can have anything I want?"

Therapist: "Hey, the sky is the limit after a screw up like that. Right, Bill?"

Bill: "Well, yeah. I guess" (noticing the therapist's gaze). "Of course, whatever you want."

Therapist: "Whatever it is, it is important that he suffer a little and you enjoy it."

Wife: "Oh, I couldn't do that. That's just not me."

Therapist: "Oh, it's fun. I will teach you. You know my wife says, 'Guilt is a terrible thing to waste.'"

8. "Praise can only help."

"The best way to encourage your spouse is frequently."
—Bobbie Vogel[43]

Pleasant words are like a honeycomb,
Sweetness to the soul
And health to the body.

—Proverbs 16:24

I sometimes think that women would be better off with a book on dog training than they would with the latest self-help book. To begin with, they would waste very little time explaining things to the dog. Secondly, they would make their requests short and behavioral: Sit, come and stay. They would make it clear when the dog would do something wrong by saying, "No." Most importantly, they would discover that the dog lives for approval and praise. So do most men.

Ten years ago, I led a group for men who were on probation for domestic violence near an industrial plant. A group member who had almost completed his time came in. He was a big man and walked in covered in mud. When it came time for him to check in and introduce himself, he said, "I can tell you new men one thing: This stuff works. I am getting love notes in my lunch box."

There was an immediate chorus of, "Hey, wait a minute. What's the deal? How did you pull that off? What are you doing? Let us in on the secret."

When the reaction died down, I added my two bits, "Hey, I have to admit I have never gotten a love note in my lunch. I want to know what you did, too."

"You remember last week when we were having that argument?" he began. "Well, when I got home from the meeting, I told her to let the oldest one watch the kids, so that we could ride around in the van and talk. She looked stunned. I had never said that. I did what you told me and kept my mouth shut and just asked her what was the matter.

"She loved it. She got on my case, but I kept saying I understood and what else. We have been honeymooning ever since."

Find out what rewards your man responds to, and when he does what pleases you, reward him. A call at work is a big reward for some men with a simple, "I love you; thanks for listening." Others may like a hug, a kiss or a verbal or written compliment, without a "but."

Michele Weiner-Davis says it well:

> After all, conventional feminist wisdom and mainstream psychotherapy have impressed upon women the need to voice their negative feelings whenever they're upset. That's why many women who have grown weary of feeling overpowered begin scrutinizing their relationships and call their partners to task every chance they get. Well, I may be the bearer of politically incorrect news, but here

goes. In reality, voicing your discontent each and every time you're displeased is a fail-safe prescription for marital-relationship disaster.[33]

9. "You have got to know when to hold them, know when to fold them..."

There are tragedies that happen every day when mental health professionals make the wrong call. I work with a lot of men who are very eager to make changes and work very hard. Sometimes, however, their wives are in counseling with a therapist who is stuck with the philosophy that "once an abuser, always an abuser. They only get worse over time. The only answer is divorce."

There are divorces that are happening needlessly in my practice right now because of this belief. Actually, one is an angry woman who has changed, but her husband and his therapist are stuck on the idea that she cannot change.

At the second National Conference on Anger, Rage and Trauma in Washington, D.C. in February 2000, one of the leading researchers on anger said to an audience of three hundred therapists that we are doing a disservice to our profession, the court system and the public by pretending that we can help all men with anger problems. There are 10 percent of angry and violent men whom we have absolutely no idea how to help and the data shows that therapy makes them worse. We need to tell the courts that we cannot help those people rather than taking the money from the probation and parole departments to treat them. Secondly, not all violence is motivated by anger. The Cobra abuser. The drive-by shooting. The bank robber. They are not necessarily suffering from an anger disorder. "A penal colony on Mars is my best answer as to what to do with them."[45]

Another book with a jarring title, *Ditch That Jerk: Dealing with Men Who Control and Hurt Women*[46] actually has some excellent criteria to use in deciding whether or not to divorce your husband or give him time to change his behavior. I recently read the criteria out loud to a female client. We quickly agreed on every answer and put her husband clearly in the "Potentially Good Man" category. Of the 17 criteria for the "Potentially Good Man" the top 3 are: 1) He is likely to use nonphysical forms of control and intimidation, such as verbal abuse; 2) he is usually employed and doesn't change jobs or get fired regularly; and 3) he does not usually have a serious alcohol or other drug problem.

It is a sad commentary when you cannot rely on a consensus of mental health professionals. When a counselor in a battered women's shelter reads in the paper about the women she works with being murdered by their husbands, she is going to be quicker to say, "Get out and divorce him." If you work with a highly motivated group of men who are mostly verbally abusive, then you are likely to see errors made when women divorce too quickly, even when the man really has made a change.

There are no disagreements on some things. First, if he hits you or pushes you, call 911. Period. The end. Secondly, if he is taken to jail, don't bail him out. Thirdly, do not lie to get him off when the case goes to the district attorney.

The "Definitely Bad Man" (the one unlikely to change) frequently feels victimized by the world and blames everyone else for his problems. He often is moody, creates chaos around him and may isolate himself and his family. Lastly, he may have a serious problem with alcohol or other drugs.

The "Utterly Hopeless Man" (he will never change—ditch him) behaves violently, even toward animals. He totally lacks feelings and empathy. He is extremely dishonest, lying whenever it suits his purposes. Often, he is charming and highly manipulative, frequently claiming to have reformed.

In Summary...

Your beliefs are important because they can keep you stuck in a miserable situation forever. Begin to adopt the beliefs outlined here and you will begin to see things change. It will become clearer to you through experimenting with these approaches whether you should continue to train him or take him to the pound.

BELIEVE THESE THINGS:

1. "There is nothing wrong with me getting him to change."
2. "There is nothing wrong with him wanting to change to please me."
3. "It's better to figure out the solution than it is to figure out the cause."
4. "There is a better way to change the relationship than talking things out."
5. "Love and trust are two separate things."
6. "I have complete confidence in my ability to take action when needed."
7. "A little psychological pain can be a good thing."
8. "Praise can only help."
9. "You have got to know when to hold them, know when to fold them..."

QUIGMANS

"First off, we need to kill the impulse to
rip up our Anger Workbook."

CHAPTER 8

C = COMMUNICATE

COMMUNICATE THESE PRINCIPLES IN YOUR DAILY CONVERSATIONS

With the techniques in this chapter, you can practice taking charge of the boundaries of discussions. It is a good sign if he is cooperative and allows you to do that. If he does not, then he needs to make amends later for losing his temper.

1. Monitor the process. Insist on a soft volume and a nice tone.

The process is the "how" something is being said. The content is the "what" is being said. It is important to keep your focus on the process more than the content. This is your new communication mantra: "Focus on the process, not on the content." This means that you interrupt as soon as you hear his voice start to get louder or meaner. You then say quietly and softly, "Your voice is getting louder and you are talking mean." If he gets loud and argues, end the conversation.

The therapists I train are surprised by how often I will interrupt and comment on the process in a counseling session. My rule *is* that the process *is* more important than the content. This is why there are no loud arguments in my marital counseling sessions. I intervene immediately when either voice increases in volume. Sometimes I will say, "Whisper."

Charles:	"Listen, Vicky, that is not what happened."
Therapist:	"Charles, your voice is getting louder."
Charles:	"I don't care. I'm not going to sit here and let her lie about what happened."
Therapist:	"Charles, I hate to tell you, but I don't care about what happened. No married couple can ever agree on what happened. Do you think my wife and I agree on what happens? Of course not. What is important is that you become aware of when your voice starts to get louder and meaner."
Vicky:	"He is always yelling at me and the kids."
Therapist:	"Vicky, you also need to talk softly. It looks like he's not the only one with a loud voice."
Charles:	"Well, I want to explain what happened."
Therapist:	"Quietly, so I can barely hear you. First, your delusion of what happened, then her delusion. Remember there is no truth here, just two delusions. The important thing is to change the way you talk."

2. Be ready to end the conversation.

"Never go to bed angry. Stay up and fight."

—Phyllis Diller

Sometimes when I am giving a presentation, a woman in the audience will ask me, "What do I do if he is screaming, breaking furniture and threatening to kill me if I try to leave?"

My standard answer is, "I have no idea." All of my interventions are geared to taking the pot off the fire as soon as it gets warm. If it gets hot, you have waited too long. If it is boiling, you are in trouble. If it is boiling over and the grease is on fire, there are then a hundred options depending on the situation.

Sometimes I will say to my wife, "Is this conversation sounding familiar to you?" She will agree. I then say, "Is there a way to have a different kind of conversation? I am bored with this one. We've had it a hundred times. I know both your lines and my lines."

The point is to notice early the signs that the conversation has taken a wrong turn. You may want to try once to correct it, then end it. "I am sorry, honey, but I am not going to have this conversation tonight. Let's give it a rest and try it again tomorrow evening."

Most likely, your spouse is not going to say, "Oh, great idea."

He is more likely to say, "Why don't you want to talk about it?" or "Okay, but I want to tell you just this one thing."

According to John Gottman, despite what many therapists will tell you, you don't have to resolve your major marital conflicts for your marriage to thrive.[47]

3. Don't expect him to bring up major issues.

Gottman argues that more than 80 percent of the time, it's the wife who brings up sticky marital issues, while the husband tries to avoid discussing them. This isn't a symptom of a troubled marriage—it's true in most happy marriages as well.

Some men are confused when their wives feel rejected by their failure to initiate discussions about the marriage. I suggest to these men that they simply ask their wives how they is feeling about the marriage. Men often react as though it were a strange and unusual idea, "How do you think of these things?"

Unless your husband is being coached by someone like me, I would suggest that you go ahead and bring up issues you want to discuss. In my men's groups, I had trouble trying to access how happy the men were in their marriages and in their lives. What we do now is go around weekly and give a score between 1 and 10 on "Marital Satisfaction" and between 1 and 10 on "Life Satisfaction." I am often shocked at the scores, which means that even though I am a trained therapist who has practiced for 25 years, I can't tell whether they are happy or not unless I ask them to score it.

4. Point out in a soft tone when he is not following his abstinence program or when you haven't heard a compliment in a few days.

Make it clear to him that you don't just want him to read the menu in the first part of this book, but you want him to order the meal, eat it and digest it. It is important that you be clear with your boundaries.

Do not harbor resentments about the way he is slipping back to his old ways. Point it out to him. This is much better than attempting to have a 20-minute conversation about "why" he is not following his program. It is better to say, "This is really important to me. I am serious. I don't want you cursing any more."

5. Better to say what you want than ask what he feels.

Asking him to share his feelings with you may be confusing to him. If you want reassurance that he still loves you, then ask. If he answers like he really doesn't mean it, then say, "Please say it like you mean it."

6. Catch him doing something right.

Be ready to share compliments with him. You may want to see if you can overdo it both in frequency and intensity. For example, some men like hearing, "You are the most wonderful husband in the world. I am so lucky I have you." For others, it's a bit much. Many, like me, just enjoy hearing them over routine tasks that I do every week. It makes me, and a lot of men, feel loved.

7. Live in "behavior land," *not* "psychology land."

Don't trust the expert's theories. Don't spend too much time analyzing and psychologizing your marriage. Some women believe that they can never be happy unless their husband becomes committed to years of exploring himself.

It is really okay for you to live in *psychology land*. In fact, I have lived there most of my life. The problem starts when I drag my wife into it with discussions about what I think her motivation is for doing something.

There can be a happy marriage for you in *behavior land*, by saying what you like and by asking for what you want in behavioral terms.

In Summary...

Some of us men can catch on early that what we are doing with our anger is not working. It certainly has nothing to do with our level of education. I recently saw an inspiring young man under 30. He said, "You know, I have never read a book. I dropped out of school in the ninth grade, but if you have a book on anger, I'm going to read it!" Some of us men are too smart and too educated to let go of our inflated idea of ourselves and admit that what we are doing is not only not working for us but is wrong.

When the pupil is ready, the teacher will appear. When your husband is ready, the concepts of abstaining will be a relief to him. He will be excited to have something specific on which he can *focus*. He will be even more excited to discover that he can do it. If an angry man has religious beliefs, he may begin to see how he has not been living up to them with his anger and self-righteousness. The concepts of humility and kindness will be attractive to him and he will have a way to put them into practice through some specific behaviors.

Through new ways of communicating, an angry man can express his humility and kindness. He can express it in his tone and the volume of his voice. He can thank his wife with sincerity and apologize if his voice starts to climb in volume.

The women who love angry men can develop a plan for themselves to see if their man can be awakened and motivated to try a new way of life. Some men are sound asleep and show no signs of beginning to wake up. They may later in life, but not now. There are ways to figure that out.

There are women who, with quiet voices and without a word of profanity, turn their pit bulls into cocker spaniels. First you get his attention. Then you make him behave through rewards and punishments. Dogs don't understand sentences and men often don't understand paragraphs. You may need a professional trainer, like a therapist.

GUIDELINES FOR EFFECTIVE COMMUNICATION WITH ANGRY PARTNERS:

1. Monitor the process. Insist on a soft volume and a nice tone.

2. Be ready to end the conversation.

3. Don't expect him to bring up major issues.

4. Point out in a soft tone when he is not following his abstinence program or when you haven't heard a compliment in a few days.

5. Better to say what you want than ask what he feels.

6. Catch him doing something right.

7. Live in "behavior land," not "psychology land."

CONCLUSION

You Can Live Happily Together

Congratulations! You have just read a book detailing an anger-management strategy that has helped thousands of men overcome their anger problems. You have read about 15 important behaviors for you to abstain from. You have also read about 20 belief-based principles that will move you toward your goal of peace, happiness and permanent change. Lastly, you have read about learning a somewhat foreign language to help you communicate better with your spouse or partner. These phrases are difficult to master at first. Every angry man will feel awkward when trying on this new language, but soon it will sound more natural.

Lifestyles of the Happily Married

Some things never get discussed in self-help books. One of the things I am reluctant to mention is alcohol consumption because it often triggers such defensiveness about how little and how infrequently people drink.

In therapy, I sometimes gingerly point out that the last three really bad arguments the couple had occurred on the way home from parties where they both had been drinking. Many couples go on for years trying to work things out when it is apparent to others that as long as they drink, they will fight.

It should be no secret to rageaholic men that alcohol is not going to improve their problem. Those with anger problems need all the self-control they can get. Taking any substance that lessens that control will increase their chances of losing their temper. When men are pushing me with the question, "What else can I do not to lose my temper again?" I tell them to stop drinking. It is certainly not going to hurt your recovery from anger. I tell men who drink, "You may be one of those people, like me, who have to choose between drinking and marriage. It became obvious that I couldn't do both."

The data on marijuana now is also clear that it releases inhibition and does not help impulsive, angry people. No drug taking or drinking helps. If anger is a problem in your marriage, you could help yourself and the marriage by completely abstaining from any substance that disinhibits your behaviors.

Fatigue is also an underemphasized element in anger. As a society, we are working more and sleeping less, then we puzzle over why our society is becoming angrier. Just like I can't drink and stay married, I can't work 80 hours a week and stay married. Sleeping is an important part of staying on course with your anger-recovery program. I sleep like people slept 100 hundred years ago, about nine hours a night. I am in a good mood when I sleep like that. Those of you who are working rotating shifts are prone to more fatigue and will have to work harder to keep adjusting to different sleep schedules.

Moderate exercise like walking helps reduce anger. Intense competitive sports make it worse.[48] A vigorous 30-minute walk, six days a week, adds to your health and decreases your anger. If you don't have young children, then you can walk together while you talk. Some of the lifestyle issues that can support a happy marriage are sleep, exercise and sobriety.

Satisfaction

Remember Jim R. from Chapter 1? He is the 65-year-old man who was arrested for assaulting his granddaughter. His wife left him and his adult children were not speaking to him.

I telephoned for Jim, but when his wife, Lattie, answered, I identified myself.

Lattie: "Oh, Newton. Jim has been so sweet to me."

Therapist: "Sweet? I must have reached the wrong number."

Lattie: "No, I mean it. I had surgery, as you know, two months ago and he has stayed home the whole time and taken care of me. He has not lost his temper or said one cross word to me. Thank you so much for helping him."

Therapist:	"You are welcome. I am glad you are happy with our work. You know he hasn't been able to come to group since your surgery, so I wanted to find out if he is ready to come back. By your report, however, it sounds like he is cured."
Lattie:	"I know he misses coming. I will have him call you when he gets back."

A few hours later:

Jim:	"Hi, Newton, I am returning your call."
Therapist:	"I was just checking to see if you are coming back to group."
Jim:	"I could probably leave Lattie alone next week. Could I come back on Tuesday?"
Therapist:	"Sure. By the way, it sounds like you are doing great. Lattie said that you have been so-o-o-o sweet and have not had one outburst."
Jim:	"Hey, don't tell the guys in the group about the "sweet" part. It hasn't been easy. Probably the most difficult thing I ever did."
Therapist:	"Do you think you really need to come back to the group?"
Jim:	"To be realistic, yes. I am the most dangerous when I think I have the problem solved. I think two more months should do it unless I have some major slip."

Graduating from Anger Group "with Honors"

There is a couple I have stayed in contact with through the years and they have continued to do well. John is a great example of someone not believing in the ABC method, but trying it anyway since he did not know what else to do.

John and Dorothy are a couple in their mid-30s. They have two young children. When they came in for the first visit, they reported that they had been separated for over a year. During that time, each had hired very expensive and well-known attorneys and had spent $100,000 each on a custody fight over the children. They both very tentatively agreed to go back to counseling and give it one more try. Several other therapists had *referred them to me as the marriage counselor who works with very difficult cases. John joined one of my men's groups and after a few meetings, he spoke to a new member, Jerry.*

John: "Listen, the first time I came into this office with my wife, I was shocked. Newton would hardly let either one of us talk. He kept saying to me, "I don't care what you think the problem is with your wife. We all have problems. Tell me three things you really like about her." I had spent the last year waging all-out legal war on my wife. I had attacked her at every weakness I could think of. It was a change to start thinking about what I did like about her and begin to focus on her positive qualities.

"Listen, Jerry, I would advise you to do the same thing. All I hear you doing is making a brilliant analysis of her problems."

Jerry: "I appreciate your feedback, but I don't see how things can get any better unless she makes some changes too."

John: "You may be like me. If you can't shut up and give in to her wishes some of the time, you may not have a chance."

Jerry: "How long did this take? I don't have forever. She has already filed you know."

John: "All the damage done with the two families and friends took months to heal."

Jerry: "Would you say you are happy now?"

John: "We have been back living together for 18 months now. I am satisfied and happy in my marriage 70 percent of the time, which is pretty good I think."

Jerry: "Aren't you worried that it could come unraveled again? I mean, I don't think I could go through this again."

John: "I would say that we are both calm now and hopeful about the future."

Jerry: "But I don't know what to do."

John: (laughing) "You mean you don't like what you are going to have to do to save your marriage. I'm sure Newton already told you. When you are angry, 'Shut up.' Instead of arguing, say, 'You are right,' and mean it.

"You now have the tools to stop raging and you never have to rage again. These methods will work today and for the rest of your life. You now know that if you are a rageful man it is time for you to wake up, shut up and grow up. You have a method to get from 'right' to happily married.

Saying "No" Without Anger

Sometimes the answer is "no" and it doesn't make your wife happy. How do you say "no" in a way that creates the least amount of damage and resentment?

This scenario may look familiar to you. See how Charles does it:

Sarah: "Honey, I hope you haven't forgotten that we are going to Mary's wedding this Saturday afternoon."

Charles can't remember her ever mentioning the wedding. He didn't even know Mary had a boyfriend. Charles distinctly remembers telling Sarah that he and three other buddies were going fishing. He had arranged the trip and put down the deposit with a guide that is hard to book. So what does Charles say? "There ain't no way; you can forget it?" No, he is smarter than that.

Charles: "Oh, no. That is Saturday? Oh, no, this is a terrible thing. I don't know what we are going to do."

Sarah: "What are you talking about?"

Charles: "This is the weekend the guys and I are going on that fishing trip."

Sarah: "That's not fair. That's not right. You made a commitment a month ago. You gave me your word. This is important to me. How could you forget? You're going to embarrass me by not being there."

Working on a good relationship and working on not getting angry are not always about doing what the other person wants you to do. Sometimes in the real world, there are going to be misunderstandings and angry feelings. It doesn't always mean that you have made a mistake if your wife gets mad at you. It doesn't necessarily mean that you have done anything wrong if she says what you are doing is unfair. The goal is to avoid escalating the discussion into an argument. Two of your mottoes by now are 1) talk in a soft voice and 2) say the three magic words.

> **Charles:** "You are right. This is a terrible situation. You are right. This is a horrible mess."

[Do not bring up past situations where she has not kept her word. Do not argue the point that you told her, and that she is the one who is wrong. Soft voice, three magic words, and now empathy.]

> **Charles:** "I know Mary is a good friend of yours and it is going to be embarrassing for you to go alone."
>
> **Sarah:** "Does that mean you are going?"
>
> **Charles:** "No. I am already committed to this trip. Is there any way for me to make this up to you?"
>
> **Sarah:** "No. This is horrible. You are breaking your word to me again. I can't believe this. Why can't you break your plans?"
>
> **Charles:** "Honey, I can't. I know this is important to you. I love you. I will make it up to you, if you will just tell me how."

Charles still goes fishing. It really doesn't matter who is right or wrong. The example is just to illustrate the value of damage control when there is hurt. Charles knows it is going to be bad from the beginning. Notice that he does NOT have to get angry to say no.

If you have an anger problem, you need to be practicing for the next time. Remind yourself to keep a soft voice, say the three magic words, empathize and reassure.

Resentments

If you are the one with the anger problem, I encourage you not to share your resentments right away. However, if a day later you still have the resentments after working to dissolve them, and you believe it might be better to share them, then structure is your friend.

First, structure the time. Do not start free-form at 10:00 p.m. and keep going until 3:00 a.m. Ask for 20 minutes and set your watch. Then I suggest that you swap resentments so that one person is not listening for a long period of time.

Person one begins by saying, "I resent you for 'X'" ('X' equals one short sentence).

Person two mirrors exactly: "I understand that you resent me for 'X'."

Person two sends: "I resent you for 'Y'" ('Y' equals one brief statement).

Person one says: "I understand that you resent me for 'Y.'"

As simple and mechanical as this process seems, it can be very difficult if your spouse is saying something you absolutely do not agree with. It is hard to keep it in your mind long enough to repeat it.

Warning: Do not get off the track and discuss the issues. End the discussion at 20 minutes and do not return to any of the topics for 24 hours. Many experts in the field of marriage and family therapy believe that 80 percent of problems can be resolved by just "being heard." Frequently, "problem-solving" isn't even needed when active listening is practiced.

No Agreement

Most couples try to discuss solutions before all the feelings are aired out around the topic. If the feelings can be shared and heard in a respectful way, clients have less invested in having the outcome be exactly their way.

Let us say that you have a daughter, Susan, who just turned 16 and your wife just took her to get her driver's license. She has a party this weekend in the evening, but you don't think she should be driving after dark yet. Your wife thinks you are being ridiculous.

First, air out in a structured way by sharing resentments about anything connected to this issue. What kind of feelings do you have about Susan's maturity and her judgment? What kind of resentments do you have toward your wife about things in the past that she has done related to giving Susan or other kids too much freedom? What are your worries?

Without trying to solve the problem or argue over who is right, first listen to the other's feelings and mirror back what they say. Do not debate or argue.

The next step is for one of you to be a secretary and write down all the possible ideas you have without evaluating any of them as you go. This would include the ridiculous. Buy her a car tomorrow. Hire a limousine and a driver. Let her go just this time, but one of you follow her to see how she does. Let her go this time, but next week spend more time on a policy. Research to see what other parents are doing. Do not let her go this week and discuss it some more next week. Do not evaluate your ideas.

Unless it is critical, wait a day and go through them one at a time and discuss them. Then when you are through with the list, see if you agree or can compromise.

Do people really do this? I do. It takes less time than having circular arguments that go around and around for days, where each person gets more and more committed to his or her position.

There is an escape from macho prison. You do not have to stay there for the rest of your life. Remember, angry men can find happiness too: Abstain, Believe and Communicate.

Wake up.

   Shut up.

      Grow up.

There is a way out of macho prison.

EPILOGUE

There have been many additional blessings since I got serious about getting my own anger under control. One of the gifts has been not having to be so controlling in other areas of my life. Recently, my wife and I went to dinner and a movie. For some reason she got in the driver's seat. I decided not to comment on this but to just get in and ride. I found it to be very pleasant. Every time we stopped for dinner, movie, coffee or to shop for CDs, I expected her to ask me to drive. She never did. We had a great day and I did not have to struggle to contain myself.

A few years ago I was in a new members class at a church. I dropped out of the class for several reasons. A few weeks later the associate pastor of the church called and said he wanted to go to lunch with me. I agreed. When the time came, I knew he was going to ask me about why I quit coming to his church and dropped out of the new members class. I decided I would use this time to ask him a deep spiritual question: "What does it mean to turn your will and your life over to God and just how do you do that?"

After we dispensed with his questions about my being a dropout, I asked him my question. His answer surprised me. He said that he did not know about turning his will over to God in an abstract way, that he had to make it more specific. What he would do would be to choose a weekend to turn his will over to his wife without telling her. He would ask what she wanted to do all weekend and try to follow her wishes the best he could. This was his method. He said, "I may not be turning my will over to God, but I am at least practicing getting out of my will. I trust her enough that I don't think I will be doing anyone any harm."

I thought about this man recently. How surprised I was to hear a man in a clerical collar talk about such a practical way of getting out of his will for a two-day period.

I thought back six years ago to how scary and radical this idea seemed to me. Yesterday, though, I had let my wife decide on the movie, the time of the movie, the restaurant, the coffee house, the CD store, when it was time to go home as well as who was driving the car. All of this I thought of in retrospect.

This morning was different. I didn't have the whole day to play. She made several requests. I said, "I am not going to have time to do any of that. I have to get to the office as soon as possible."

This morning I also made a comment about the process along with a request. She had said, "I am sorry *if* I was rude to you earlier. I was on the phone."

I commented that it would please me more when she apologized if she said, "I apologize *for* being rude to you earlier."

Her response was: "Was I rude?"

I said, "Yeah."

I find it a miracle that I can follow one day, say no and make a request the next day...all without anger! What a relief it is to know that I can follow, rather than always leading and having things "the right way." I have spent most of my life thinking that leadership is good and following is bad. There are all kinds of books on how to be a leader. There are *few* books on helping us to follow more comfortably. I want to follow the principles of kindness and mercy at the heart of all great religions. I want to follow the advice of elders whom I trust and admire. I want to follow the wisdom found in the scriptures and sacred stories.

The ability to think for myself, to blaze my own path, and to lead the way for others, is only valuable if I also have the ability to follow a path of spiritual principles. If I compulsively need to lead, I will lead myself into ego and anger trouble.

APPENDIX A

COUNSELING WITH ANGRY MEN

"Most men get to counseling with the footprint of a woman on their rear end."

—Newton Hightower

Court-Ordered Groups:

Can Mandated Therapy Be Effective?

Some men are sent to groups by the court as part of their probation for domestic violence. Many of these groups are connected with battered women's shelters. In most parts of the country, these programs are based on the Duluth Model, which emphasizes the need for men to be re-socialized about their sexist ideas about women. If your husband is on probation with required classes, he is usually motivated to attend the classes or counseling sessions. The classes are *his* worries, not yours. Remember, it is not a good sign of progress to be more worried about him violating his probation for nonattendance than he is. A sign of progress in the relationship is when you do *not* call around to find out about the classes; he does. If the program he attends has a group for women or couples, by all means attend. It improves the chances of meaningful change if both of you attend. Don't worry if he doesn't like it. He doesn't have to like it for it to be useful.

Now, what if he is not a physical abuser, but you know that he needs some help? There used to be a myth that change could happen in therapy only if a person was motivated to go on his or her own. Have you heard the joke about how many therapists it takes to change a light bulb? One, but the light bulb really has to want to change. The humor typifies this "old myth" assumption.

The maxim, "You can lead a horse to water, but you can't make it drink," certainly applies. However, I have seen again and again that mandated counseling is a critical part of creating that thirst for change.

Choosing a Counselor

"There are so many therapists in the yellow pages. How do I pick the right one?"

First Guideline. The first guideline in choosing a therapist or counselor is that *you don't want to go to someone who believes the myth that mandated therapy doesn't work.* I have run a very full practice of effective men's groups for many years. Not once has someone called and said, "You know, I just woke up this morning and decided that it was time to do something about my anger problem." It is usually, "I am about to lose my wife," or "I am about to lose my job." Fear is a great motivator.

Second Guideline. The second criterion for an effective therapist is that *he or she not be concerned with whether your husband believes in therapy or not.* If someone is skeptical about therapy, he will focus more on *results.* A modest view of therapy is the safest. Find a therapist who will tell you specifically what to expect, without making grandiose promises.

Third Guideline. The therapist should be willing to give you some advice about how to get your husband into therapy. The phrases I suggest are, "I don't care if you don't want to go"; "You may be right"; "It may be a waste of money"; "I want you to go. The appointment is tomorrow at 10:00 a.m." I encourage wives to keep saying the previous statements over and over like a broken record until they get agreement—unless, of course, the husband tends toward violence. Then she might want to see the therapist alone to get a coaching session on how to get him in.

Fourth Guideline. Avoid therapists who immediately take the position that your husband is dangerous and will only get worse over time—that is, unless he *is* dangerous. If he has put you into the emergency room twice, and hurt his former wife, then you do need to get into therapy to get help for yourself. *If he is a verbal abuser and the therapist wants you to ditch him immediately, then I would suggest you ditch the therapist instead.*

Fifth Guideline. Avoid therapists who psychologically diagnose your husband from afar. Typically, the "dump him" diagnosis is "Antisocial Personality Disorder." Incidentally, if he comes home from his therapist with a diagnosis for you of "Borderline Personality Disorder" that means his therapist may think you need to be dumped. These are what I call the two "Psycho-Nasties." Typically when wives ask me for a diagnosis of their angry husband, whether he is in the room or not, I tell them he sounds like a "chronic jerk" to me. When they ask what the goal of therapy is, I tell them to make him a "recovering jerk" like me. Most men I see are clear that they need to quit acting like jerks or they are going to divorce court.

First Session

It is important that whomever you see for therapy, makes an assessment of your husband for specific psychological problems that respond well to medication, often drastically reducing anger outbursts. For instance, in the initial session, I have men take a five-minute written depression and anxiety test. Typically, men are more honest on paper and pencil tests than in face-to-face interviews. I have them score the tests themselves and tell me what they scored. If the client is in a range of anxiety or depression that could respond well to medication, I refer him to a psychiatrist for medication evaluation, and have him take the tests with him to the appointment. A short written test for anxiety and depression can be found in the *Feel Good Handbook*, by David Burns, M.D.[49]

A psychiatrist is a medical doctor who specializes in prescribing medication for people with anxiety, depression, rage, anger or other psychological problems. Using your family doctor may be okay, but it is not likely he works with a lot of patients with anger problems. A psychiatrist will do a thorough evaluation. It may take two or three tries to get the medication right.

APPENDIX B

ANGRY MEN AND MEDICATION

by David C. Kay, M.D.

Dr. Kay is currently Medical Director for the Center for Anger Resolution, Inc. He was Chief of the Experimental Psychiatry Unit at the Addiction Research Center in Lexington, Kentucky for 20 years, and director of the Houston VA Medical Center inpatient substance abuse unit for 7 years. Dr. Kay has extensive experience in prescribing medications for patients with anger disorders, and has published on his research in psychotropic medications. He has been in private practice in Houston since 1985.

Anger and Medications: Where Do Medications Fit Into the Picture of Working on Anger?

Joe was at his wits end. He just blew up again at his wife after they tried to talk about getting back together. They had been separated for three months. Just like she always did, his wife had said something and Joe just felt his head get big and hot. The next thing you know, he grabbed her by the throat. His life went down the drain again.

When his therapist sent Joe in to see the psychiatrist, it came to light that he had a history since childhood of being hyperactive and of having his thoughts go fast. He always spoke fast and was restless. Although some of his symptoms got better, the one that had grown worse over time was his easily-triggered temper. He had been in lots of fights growing up, as part of proving that he was a tough guy. He currently works in construction and occasionally gets into physical fights with some of his co-workers.

His relationship with his wife has suffered most from Joe's anger. Joe is an example of someone who has had a growth in anger throughout his life. Joe's anger decreased when he started on a mood stabilizer called lithium. He then found that he could listen to his "provocative" wife and deal with her differently so that they were able to get back together again. Lithium was part of the answer that allowed him to set up a new kind of relationship with the help of their therapist.

Mike is a different example. Mike is a person who has had trouble keeping his attention on things. In recent years, his therapist figured out that he had Attention Deficit Disorder (ADD). He certainly met the criteria, because Mike was forever starting things and never finishing them, jumping from one thing to another.

It seemed appropriate that Ritalin would be used for Mike as an adult ADD patient. However, when he began taking Ritalin, instead of just correcting his attention problem, it made it more likely that he would explode into anger. He was then switched over to Adderall and found that both of these stimulants made his anger problem worse. He said that, thanks to the medication, he was really going to be able to concentrate as he read his divorce papers. He needed to take a medication for his anger in addition to his Adderall. In Mike's case, the addition of a Selective Serotonin Reuptake Inhibitor (SSRI) anti-depressant quieted down his tendency for anger and allowed the stimulant effect of the Adderall to do its job. He was able to take the two medications and get a benefit from them together. Men with severe anger problems and severe ADD often have to be monitored by a psychiatrist for many months in order to get the medication adjusted correctly.

John is a man of many moods, mostly dark. When he gets into a particularly depressed episode, he gets very irritable and the least little thing will send him into a rage. He feels very apologetic later and feels even worse about himself for behaving in such a way. For John, the antidepressant that helped him the most was Wellbutrin, one that increased his energy as well as his mood and enabled him to move out of anger as a method of handling his depression.

There are two major types of anger that need to be addressed when seeking medical treatment. First, there is *primary anger*. A person with primary anger is like a car in which the motor is running fast all the time. This is the kind of individual who has been "on-the-go" ever since childhood.

This patient's anger results primarily when somebody thwarts his desire to get something done, because this is a man who always wants to be doing something. Anything that gets in his way leads to anger to overcome that obstacle. One of the problems, of course, is that oftentimes anger *is* effective in overcoming obstacles, so there is a tendency for this person to begin using it for dealing with all sorts of things in his life.

Secondary anger occurs in all of us when we use anger, consciously or unconsciously, to overcome weak feelings such as fear, shame or sadness. For some people, getting angry becomes part of the solution to dealing with any "bad" feelings. Individuals who are afraid that they're going to be deserted get angry. They also get angry when they feel smothered. They become angry when somebody embarrasses them by a comment they make or an insight they have. The problem for individuals who have secondary anger is that dealing just with the angry feelings is not adequate. The ability to analyze the anger (i.e., "What was I thinking just before I got angry?") and find that your anger quiets down when you diminish fears, shame and sad thoughts; this characterizes that anger as secondary.

What medical diagnoses might a rageaholic receive?

The first diagnosis that needs to be considered for a man who rages is manic-depressive or bipolar disorder, with its lesser variant of cyclothymia. These are individuals whose anger tends to be primary, although they can certainly have secondary anger as a method for dealing with many other feelings in their lives. When these individuals get hyperactive, they are more likely to go into a rage, so they are not continuously raging but episodically raging with a normal mood or a depressed mood at other times.

Major depressive disorder, or unipolar depressive disorder, is a diagnosis that includes many men who rage, but when looking at the background out of which they rage, you will discover that it's when their depression gets severe that they explode into anger as a way of handling it.

The third major category in which rage is seen is in drug abusers. While working with drug abusers at the VA hospital, we discovered that they tend to neglect, ignore or avoid all sorts of negative feelings, except anger. They are oriented around either getting excited by doing something dangerous or getting angry when they try to deal with negative feelings.

The treatment unit was often hectic with individuals yelling and demonstrating their competency to dispense verbal abuse. As would be expected, a certain number of these individuals had problems with being manic depressive, cyclothymic or depressed. There were particular problems with individuals who were alcoholics. The alcohol lowered the inhibitions of their anger, but also provided an amnesia of the rage afterward. Consequently, they didn't feel guilty about it. Stimulants, including amphetamines and cocaine, are also known to produce rages because they increase irritability and can give the user paranoid thoughts that everyone is out to hurt them.

A recent problem in terms of rage, has been the overdiagnosing and overprescribing of adult Attention Deficit Disorder, in which Ritalin is proposed as the cure. However, one of the characteristics that stimulants like Ritalin have is that they will make anger and rage more likely in susceptible individuals. Besides these four major categories of men who rage, there are other problems that are less frequent, including Intermittent Explosive Disorder, rage in individuals who are mentally retarded, and sudden rage and violence in individuals who have had prior head injury.

What are the advantages and disadvantages of medications for anger?

A. Neuroleptics: Ever since Thorazine was found to subdue dangerous wild animals, this class of medications has been called "tranquilizers." They likewise can help a raging man to quiet down quickly. Thorazine, Stelazine, Trilafon, Prolixin, Haldol, and Mellaril have all been helpful drugs, but their use has decreased in recent years because they have sometimes produced Tardive Dyskinesia (TD), an unwanted and sometimes permanent movement disorder. All neuroleptics were thought to do this until Clozaril (a highly useful but highly toxic neuroleptic) was found to produce no TD. Modern neuroleptics are being developed to be more like Clozaril without its toxicity, and are called atypical neuroleptics. Risperdal is an atypical neuroleptic with less toxicity though, like the older neuroleptics, it tends to increase sleep while increasing appetite and decreasing sexual function. Seroquel is the atypical neuroleptic most useful for sleep. It works well with the elderly since it has the least chance of increasing delirium or dementia. Zyprexa significantly increases appetite. All neuroleptics are very effective in quickly decreasing anger and rage.

B. Mood stabilizers: In 1946 Cade discovered that lithium would calm mania. It now is known that lithium will calm other hyperactive states including rage and anger. In recent years, a group of anticonvulsants have been found to stabilize mood. They all slow rapid thoughts and rapid talk. They quiet restlessness and decrease anger. Most mood stabilizers (lithium, Depakote, Tegretol, Neurontin) increase appetite, except for Topamax, which decreases appetite, and Trileptal and Lamictal, which are reported to be weight-neutral.

C. SSRI antidepressants: Selective Serotonin Reuptake Inhibitors work mostly on serotonin receptors to decrease depression. All five, (Prozac, Zoloft, Paxil, Luvox and Celexa), tend to decrease appetite at first, but later gradually increase it in some people. All of these decrease sexual function, though Luvox might have less of that effect. They have a variable effect on sleep, and decrease anger that is secondary to anxiety or depression.

D. Atypical antidepressants: Wellbutrin increases energy, decreases sleep, decreases appetite and increases sexual function. Effexor increases energy, decreases sleep, decreases and then increases appetite, and decreases sexual function. Serzone increases sleep, decreases appetite, and doesn't decrease sexual function. Remeron increases sleep, increases appetite and doesn't decrease sexual function. All of these antidepressants also decrease anger secondary to anxiety or depression. All antidepressants have a gradual onset to their antidepressant effects, with Effexor being the fastest and Prozac being the slowest. All SSRI and atypical antidepressants tend to increase primary anger, and tend to decrease secondary anger.

Besides prescribed medications that decrease rage, there are drugs of abuse that have been used by individuals to try to get a handle on rage. It has been found that individuals who abuse alcohol, sedative-hypnotics, stimulants and hallucinogens actually can see a worsening of their rage, while some see a decrease in rage with the use of marijuana or morphine-like drugs such as heroin. However, all of the drugs of abuse end up with the individual feeling worse afterward, despite temporary help with a problem like rage. There is a tendency toward increased depression in these individuals over time. A word needs to be said particularly about the sedative-hypnotics including alcohol, Valium, Librium, Ambien, Xanax and Tranxene. All of these medications have a characteristic of disinhibiting the user's behavior. Trouble begins when the disinhibition by the medications takes over.

Why is medication a hard pill to swallow for some men?

There are many reasons that some men do not like to take medications for their mood disorders, and end up discontinuing them:

1. They do not take them for a long enough period (a month to six weeks) so that the side effects diminish and the positive effects begin.
2. They take too low a dose and have the experience of nothing changing.
3. They do not return to the psychiatrist for an adjustment in the medication, but just discontinue it.
4. They are uncomfortable with the occasional loss of sexual function associated with the SSRI group of medications.
5. They do not like the stigma of being the "sick one" in the marriage due to taking medication.

Why are some men eager to try medication?

There are, however, noteworthy reasons why a lot of men are eager to try medication and get good results:

1. Their wives are very pleased by their willingness to take this step.
2. They have been depressed and anxious for years and are glad to discover some help.
3. They want to do whatever they can to contain their anger outbursts and want to do everything possible to help themselves.
4. They are relieved that there is something real and identifiable that is wrong with them, rather than their just being mean or bad.

Counseling and medication may be important ingredients in breaking the anger cycle in your relationship. The counseling may involve individual therapy (typically for the man), couples counseling and/or group counseling. The experience does not have to be pleasurable, but it does need to help you change. An important adjunct that is always important for angry men to consider is appropriate medication evaluation. Medication will not "cure" angry behavior, but it may help make the behaviors "manageable" enough to learn new ones. In fact, appropriate medication may help you read all the way through this book rather than tossing it in the back yard.

Printed by permission King Syndicated Features

END NOTES

1 (p. 19) Daniel Sonkin & Michael Durphy, *Learning to Live Without Violence*, Volcano Press, 1982. This classic best-seller is now available in a revised, updated and enhanced version (1997).

2 (p. 21) For more indepth review of research on the role of hostility and chronic anger on physical health see Todd Miller & Timothy Smith, "A Meta-Analytic Review of Research on Hostility and Physical Health," *Psychological Bulletin*, March 1996, *119:2*, pp. 322-349 and an earlier, though still highly relevant review by S. Booth-Kewley & H. Friedman, "Psychological Predictors of Heart Disease: A Quantitative Review," *Psychological Bulletin*, 1987, *101*, 343-362.

3 (p. 21) Lance Morrow's provocative book (*Heart: A Memoir*, Warner Books, 1995) is a must-read for all men with heart problems. In fact, Sherwin Nuland, author of award-winning *How We Die: Reflections on Life's Final Chapter* (Vintage Books, 1994), asserts that Morrow's writing strikes an unexpectedly universal chord and is worthy reading for "all of us" facing life's challenges.

4 (p. 21) For at least the past two decades, a considerable body of research has highlighted the relationship between hostility and hypertension. For instance, research in the early 80's (e.g., C. D Jenkins, "Epidemiology of Cardiovascular Diseases," *Journal of Consulting and Clinical Psychology*, 1988, *56*, 324-332; T. M. Dembroski, et. al., "Components of Type A, Hostility and Anger-in: Relationship to Angiographic Findings," *Psychosomatic Medicine*, 1985, *47*, 219-233) is consistent with findings in the late 90's (e.g., C. M. Meesters & J. Smulders, "Hostility and Myocardial Infarction in Men," *Journal of Psychosomatic Research*, 1994, *38*, 727-734; Brandon Bunting, et. al., "A Group Comparison of Those with Hypertension and Other Chronic Illness: A Factor and Item Level Analysis of Anger and Hostility," *Psychology and Health*, 2000, *15:4*, 527-538).

5 (p. 21) For a highly readable account of Kawachi's research see "Grumpy Old Men Have a Higher Risk of Heart Disease," *Modern Medicine*, April 1997, *65:4*, pp. 57-62. For a more technical and detailed review, see I. Kawachi & D. Spiro, "A Prospective Study of Anger and Coronary Heart Disease: The Normative Aging Study," *Circulation*, November 1, 1996.

6 (p. 21) For additional investigations on the role of interpersonal expressions of anger and physical health see Jeffrey Richards, Alexandra Hof & Marlies Alvarenga, "Serum lipids and their

relationships with hostility and angry affect and behaviors in men," *Health Psychology*, July 2000, *19*, pp. 363-370 and Carrie Sargent, Stephen Flora, & Stacey Williams, "Vocal Expression of Anger and Cardiovascular Reactivity within Dyadic Interactions," *Psychological Reports*, June 1999, *84:3*, pp. 809-817.

7   (p. 32) Redford Williams & Virginia Williams, *Anger Kills*, Harper Perennial, 1994.

8   (p. 32) Carol Tavris, *Anger: The Misunderstood Emotion*, Touchstone Books, 1989.

9   (p. 33) Douglas T. Talbott, M.D., Keynote Address: "Eating Disorders and Other Addictions: A Holistic Disease." Atlanta, GA, U.S. Journal Training, Eating Disorders Conference, 1988.

10 (p. 35) Matthew 7:3-5, *New American Standard Bible*. (All scriptural references are to the *New American Standard Bible*. Foundation Press, 1971.)

11 (p. 43) Martin P. Seligman & Martin E. P. Seligman, *What You Can Change...and What You Can't*, Fawcett Books, 1995, pp. 127-128.

12 (p. 71) Alcoholics Anonymous, *Alcoholics Anonymous*, AA World Services, 1939, p. 47.

13 (p. 71) Bo Lozoff, *Deep and Simple: A Spiritual Path for Modern Times*, Human Kindness Foundation, 1999.

14 (p. 72) Alcoholics Anonymous, *The Twelve Steps and The Twelve Traditions*, AA World Services, 1953, p. 91.

15 (p. 74) Alcoholics Anonymous, *The Twelve Steps and The Twelve Traditions*, p. 98.

16 (p. 76) Alcoholics Anonymous, *The Twelve Steps and The Twelve Traditions*, p. 67.

17 (p. 77) Alcoholics Anonymous, *The Twelve Steps and The Twelve Traditions*, p. 62.

18 (p. 78) Alcoholics Anonymous, *The Twelve Steps and The Twelve Traditions*, p. 60.

19 (p. 79) *New American Standard Bible*, Matthew 25: 40.

20 (p. 79) Bo Lozoff, *Deep and Simple*, p. 67.

21 (p. 84) Bo Lozoff, *Deep and Simple*.

22 (p. 88) Excerpt printed with permission. Ram Dass & Paul Gorman, *How Can I Help?: Stories and Reflections on Service*, Alfred A. Knopf, 1985, pp 167-171.

23 (p. 91) [Letter and Reply excepted by permission from the Human Kindness Foundation Newsletter Winter 2000].

24 (p. 93) Bo Lozoff, *Deep and Simple*, p. 67.

25 (p. 94) Bo Lozoff, *Deep and Simple*, p. 68.

26 (p. 96) *NASB*, Ephesians 4:31-32.

27 (p. 97) For more fascinating history behind this classic prayer, see A Corstanje, *St. Francis Prayer Book,* Franciscan, 1978 and John Talbot, *Prayers of St. Francis,* Servant Publications, 1988.

28 (p. 109) Bill O'Hanlon, *Do One Thing Different and Other Uncommonly Sensible Solutions to Life's Persistent Problems,* William Morrow, 1999. Many of O'Hanlon's practical suggestions are directly relevant to relationships locked up by anger.

29 (p. 119) D. Moltz (1992) "Abuse and Violence: The Dark Side of the Family," in *The Journal of Marriage and Family Therapy,* p. 223.

30 (p. 120) The Department of Justice has prepared two powerful reports on violence among intimate partners: (1) *Intimate Partner Violence: Bureau of Justice Statistics Special Report.* (2000, May). Prepared by Callie Rennison & Sarah Welchans, US Department of Justice. (2) *Violence by Intimates: Analysis of Data on Crimes by Current or Former Spouses, Boyfriends, and Girlfriends.* (1998, March). Prepared by Lawrencea Greenfeld & Michael Rand, U.S. Department of Justice. These reports and other reports and data are available from the BJS Internet Web site: http://www.ojp.usdoj.gov/bjs/

31 (p. 121) See the report by Callie Rennison *Criminal Victimization 2000: Changes 1999-2000 with Trends 1993-2000.* (2001, June). Bureau of Justice Statistics—Crime Victimization Survey. U.S. Department of Justice.

32 (p. 121) The most recent, up-to-date data is available from *Injuries from Violent Crime, 1992-1998: National Crime Victimization Survey.* Prepared by Thomas Simon, James Mery, & Craig Perkins, (2001, June) with the Bureau of Justice Statistics and Center for Disease Control and Prevention. U.S. Department of Justice and U.S. Department of Health and Human Services. For other information provided by National Domestic Violence Hotline, visit the web site at: http://www.ndvh.org.

33 (p. 122) Jan Chaiken, *Crunching Numbers: Crime and Incarceration at the End of the Millennium.* National Institute of Justice Journal. (2000, January). pp. 1-17.

34 (p. 122) See Karen Stout & Beverly McPhail, *Confronting Sexism and Violence Against Women.* Addison-Wesley, 1998 for more compelling research on the impact of emotional abuse.

35 (p. 123) Domestic Abuse Intervention Project, 206 West Fourth Street, Duluth, MN 55806. 218-722-4134. [Reprinted from Karen D. Stout and Beverly McPhail, Confronting Sexism & Violence Against Women, Addison Wesley Longman, 1998.]

36 (p. 125) Lenore Walker's *The Battered Woman,* HarperCollins, 1980 has been instrumental in highlighting the violence cycle in relationships.

37   (p. 126) Neil Jacobson & John Gottman, *When Men Batter Women*, Simon & Schuster, 1998, p.36.

38   (p. 127) Neil Jacobson & John Gottman, *When Men Batter Women*, Simon & Schuster, 1998, p.36.

39   (p. 129) For a complete description of the Violence Against Women Act and for a review of state and federal regulations related to it, see the web site of the U.S. Department of Justice Violence Against Women Office (http://www.ojp.usdoj.gov/vawo/).

40   (p. 145) Michele Weiner-Davis, *A Woman's Guide to Changing Her Man: Without His Even Knowing It*, Golden Books, 1998, pp. 16-17.

41   (p. 158) John Gottman & Nan Silver, *The Seven Principles for Making Marriage Work*, Three Rivers Press, 1999, pp.113-116.

42   (p. 159) Michele Weiner-Davis, *A Woman's Guide to Changing Her Man: Without His Even Knowing It*, Golden Books, 1998, pp. 6-7.

43   (p. 161) Quoted in *How Do I Love Thee?* By Laure Ostby Kehler, p.30.

44   (p. 163) Michele Weiner-Davis, *A Woman's Guide to Changing Her Man*, p.13.

45   (p. 163) Raymond DiGiuseppe. (February, 2000). Second National Conference on Anger, Rage and Trauma. Washington, DC.

46   (p. 163) Pamela Jayne, *Ditch That Jerk: Dealing with Men Who Control and Hurt Women*, Hunter House, 2000.

47   (p. 169) J. Gottman & N. Silver, *The Seven Principles for Making Marriage Work*, p. 131.

48   (p. 174) Read the research in Williams & Williams' (1994) *Anger Kills,* for interesting data on competitive sports, anger, and life expectancy.

49   (p. 185) For more details, see David Burns, *The Feeling Good Handbook*. (1990). Plume Books.

REFERENCES

Alcoholics Anonymous. (1939). *Alcoholics Anonymous*. New York, New York: AA World Services.

Alcoholics Anonymous. (1953). *Twelve Steps and Twelve Traditions*. New York, New York: AA World Services.

Betancourt, Marian. (1997). *What to Do When Love Turns Violent: A Practical Resource for Women in Abusive Relationships*. New York, NY: Harper Perennial Library.

Berry, Dawn Bradley. (1998). *The Domestic Violence Sourcebook: Everything You Need to Know*. Los Angeles, CA: Lowell House.

Bradshaw, John. (1988). *Healing the Shame that Binds You*. Deerfield Beach, FL: Health Communications, Inc.

Burns, David. (1989). *The Feeling Good Handbook*. New York, NY: Plume Books.

Chaiken, Jan. (2000, January). *Crunching Numbers: Crime and Incarceration at the End of the Millennium*. National Institute of Justice Journal. 1-17.

Chopra, Deepak. (1995). *The Seven Spiritual Laws of Success: A Practical Guide to the Fulfillment of Your Dreams*. San Rafael, CA: Amber-Allen Publishing.

Dass, Ram and Gorman, Paul. (1985). *How Can I Help?: Stories and Reflections on Service*. New York, NY: Alfred A. Knopf.

Deschner, Jeanne. (1984). *The Hitting Habit: Anger Control for Battering Couples*. New York, NY: The Free Press.

Feshbach, Seymour. (1956). "The Catharsis Hypothesis and Some Consequences of Interaction with Aggression and Neutral Play Objects," *Journal of Personality, 24*, 449-462.

Feshbach, Seymour, Zagrodzka, Jolanta & Feshbach, Sisney (Eds.). (1997). *Aggression: Biological, Developmental, and Social Perspectives*. New York, NY: Plenum.

DiGiuseppe, Raymond. (February, 2000). Second National Conference on Anger, Rage and Trauma. Washington, DC.

Gottman, John M. and Silver, Nan. (1999). *The Seven Principles for Making Marriage Work*. New York, NY: Three Rivers Press.

Greenfeld, Lawrencea & Rand, Michael. (1998, March). *Violence by Intimates: Analysis of Data on Crimes by Current or Former Spouses, Boyfriends, and Girlfriends*. U.S. Department of Justice.

Hanh, Thich Nhat. (1991). *Peace is Every Step: The Path of Mindfulness in Everyday Life*. New York, NY: Bantam Books.

Jacobson, Neil and Gottman, John M. (1998). *When Men Batter Women: New Insights into Ending Abusive Relationships*. New York, NY: Simon & Schuster.

Jayne, Pamela. (2000). *Ditch That Jerk: Dealing with Men Who Control and Hurt Women*. Almeda, CA: Hunter House.

Justice, Blair & Justice, Rita. (1976). *The Abusing Family*. Norwell, MA: Kluwer Academic Publishers.

Lockman Foundation. (1971). *New American Standard Bible*. La Habra, Ca: Foundation Press.

Lozoff, Bo. (1999). *Deep and Simple: A Spiritual Path for Modern Times*. Durham, NC: Human Kindness Foundation.

Moltz, D. (1992). "Abuse and Violence: The Dark Side of the Family," *Journal of Marriage and Family Therapy*, p. 223.

Murphy-Milano, Susan. (1996). *Defending Our Lives: Getting Away from Domestic Violence and Staying Safe*. Landover Hills, MD: Anchor Books.

O'Hanlon, Bill. (1999). *Do One Thing Different: And Other Uncommonly Sensible Solutions to Life's Persistent Problems*. New York, NY: William Morrow.

Rennison, Callie. (2001, June). *Criminal Victimization 2000: Changes 1999-2000 with Trends 1993-2000*. Bureau of Justice Statistics—Crime Victimization Survey. U.S. Department of Justice.

Rennison, Callie & Welchans, Sarah. (2000, May). *Intimate Partner Violence: Bureau of Justice Statistics Special Report.* US Department of Justice.

Seligman, M. P. & Seligman, M.E.P. (1995). *What You Can Change...and What You Can't.* New York, NY: Fawcett Books.

Simon, Thomas; Mery, James, & Perkins, Craig. (2001, June). *Injuries from Violent Crime, 1992-1998: National Crime Victimization Survey.* Bureau of Justice Statistics and Center for Disease Control and Prevention. U.S. Department of Justice and U.S. Department of Health and Human Services.

Sonkin, Daniel & Durphy, Michael. (1982). *Learning to Live without Violence: A Handbook for Men.* Volcano, Ca: Volcano Press.

Stout, Karen & McPhail, Beverly. (1998). *Confronting Sexism and Violence Against Women: A Challenge for Social Work.* New York, NY: Addison-Wesley.

Talbott, Douglas T., M.D. (1988). Keynote Address: "Eating Disorders and Other Addictions: A Holistic Disease."

Tavris, Carol. (1989). *Anger: The Misunderstood Emotion.* New York, NY: Touchstone Books.

Walker, Lenore. (1980). *The Battered Woman.* New York, NY: HarperCollins.

Weiner-Davis, Michele. (1998). *A Woman's Guide to Changing Her Man: without his even knowing it.* New York, NY: Golden Books.

Williams, Redford & Virginia. (1994). *Anger Kills: Seventeen Strategies for Controlling the Hostility That Can Harm Your Health.* New York, NY: Harper Perennial Library.

Index

203

criticizing 65
cursing and profanity 50
interrupting 49
lecturing 65
mean tone of voice 55
mocking 58
name-calling 52
non-affectionate touching 61
pointing 55
raising your voice 55
rolling your eyes 63
sarcasm 58
sighing 63
slamming doors 59
speaking 44
staring 48
staying 46
telling hero stories 62
threatening 53
yelling 55
believing 11, 18, 19, 23, 24, 29, 33,
    38, 44, 54, 69, 70, 71, 74, 84,
    98, 102, 108, 111, 145, 175, 180
bipolar disorder 189
blood pressure 21
borderline personality disorder 185
Bradshaw, John 27, 104
brain chemistry 21
brain hemorrhages 21
build-up/blow-up 28, 29
Burns, David 185

C

careerism 92
Cartoons
    Hagar the Horrible 118, 148, 193
    Quigmans 166
    Rubes 42
catalyst 19, 158
catharsis 29, 32
cathartic 32
cathartic experience 30
cathartic expression 29
CBSSW phrases 105, 106
Celexa 191
cerebral arteriosclerosis 21
Chopra, Deepak 74
Clozaril 190
clucking 63, 64, 68
clucking (see *behaviors to abstain from*)
Cobra 163

Cobras 126, 127, 130, 133
cocaine 190
Cole, Charles 21
Colorado State University 21
communicating 18, 38, 101, 152,
    167, 171, 180
communication 173
compassion (See Principles to Practice)
compulsion 33
*Confronting Sexism and Violence
    Against Women* 122
Congress 129
contentedness 93
craving 32, 33, 35
critical 99, 113
criticism 65, 66, 72, 75, 91, 102, 113
criticizing 45, 65, 66, 68, 75, 77, 78,
    106, 113
criticizing (see *behaviors to abstain
    from*)
cursing 50, 51, 52, 56, 57, 60, 62,
    68, 95, 96, 102, 153, 170
cursing (see *behaviors to abstain from*)
cyclothymia 189

D

D Day 145
*Deep and Simple: A Spiritual Path for
    Modern Times* 71
deep doghouse communication 101,
    105, 106
deep in the doghouse 101, 102, 103,
    104, 105, 110, 111, 112
delirium 190
dementia 190
denial 32, 34, 35
Depakote 191
Department of Psychiatry and Neurolo-
    gy 21
depressed women 67, 107, 158
depressive disorder
    unipolar 189
Deschner, Jeanne 19, 20
destructive 28, 52, 90
destructive anger 25
destructive aspects of anger 20
discipline 79, 80
*Ditch That Jerk: Dealing with Men
    Who Control and Hurt Women* 163
divorce 18, 20, 23, 24, 51, 57, 67,
    69, 83, 91, 101, 107, 111, 125,

Photo by Ben Smuz

Newton Hightower

at t ... : Drugs as Factors in
Vio ... frequent speaker at
nati ... s as well as T.V. and
radi

... th anger, depression
and ... e men's groups that
meet ... of hope to men who
suffe ... ast 10 years he has
been ... ams: "I am happily
marri

T ... *ng* call 1-877-NO-
ANG ... oach Training Program[1] ... *rtified Anger Reso-
lution* .... or to receive a free monthly e-mail newsletter,
contact the Center for Anger Resolution, Inc. by phone, fax, e-mail
or on the web.

The Center for Anger Resolution, Inc.
2524 Nottingham • Houston, TX 77005-1412
Ph: (713) 526-6650
Toll Free: (877) NO-ANGER
Fax: (713) 526-4342
E-mail: info@angerbusters.com
Web site: http://angerbusters.com

ORDERING INFORMATION

Additional copies of ***Anger Busting 101: New ABCs for Angry Men and the Women Who Love Them*** are available from the publisher. Orders may be placed by phone, by mail, by FAX, or directly on the web. Purchase orders from institutions are welcome.

❑ *To order by mail:* Complete this order form and mail it (along with check, money order or credit card information) to Bayou Publishing, 2524 Nottingham, Houston, TX 77005-1412.

❑ *To order by phone:* Call (800) 340-2034.

❑ *To order by FAX:* Fill out this order form (including credit card information) and fax to (713) 526-4342.

❑ *To place a secure online order:* Visit http://www.bayoupublishing.com.

Name: _____

Address: _____

_____

City: _____ ST: ___ Zip: ____

Ph: _____

FAX: _____

❑ VISA   ❑ MasterCard   ❑ American Express

Charge Card #: _____

Expiration Date: _____

Signature: _____

Please send me ____ copies at $14.95 each _____

Sales Tax 6.25%(Texas residents) _____

plus $4.00 postage and handling *(per order)* ____ $4.00

Total $ _____

Bayou Publishing
2524 Nottingham, Suite 150
Houston, TX 77005-1412
Ph: (713) 526-4558/ FAX: (713) 526-4342
Orders: (800) 340-2034
http://www.bayoupublishing.com